YORK NOTES

General Editors: Professor A.N. Jeffares (*University of Stirling*) & Professor Suheil Bushrui (*American University of Beirut*)

Alice Walker

THE COLOR PURPLE

Notes by Neil McEwan

MA, B LITT (OXFORD) PH D (STIRLING)

Professor of English, Okayama University, Japan

LONGMAN YORK PRESS

YORK PRESS
Immeuble Esseily, Place Riad Solh, Beirut.

LONGMAN GROUP UK LIMITED
Longman House, Burnt Mill, Harlow,
Essex CM20 2JE, England
Associated companies, branches and representatives
throughout the world

© Librairie du Liban 1992

First published 1992
Third impression 1993

ISBN 0-582-09641-3

Phototypeset by Gem Graphics, Trenance, Mawgan Porth, Cornwall
Produced by Longman Singapore Publishers Pte Ltd
Printed in Singapore

Contents

Part 1

Introduction

The author's life

Alice Malsenior Walker was born in 1944 in Eatonton, Georgia, in the Deep South of the United States, the youngest child of a sharecropper (a tenant farmer who supplies a share of his crop to the landlord in place of rent). An accident blinded her in one eye when she was eight. She has said that she became more shy, thoughtful and studious as a result, and began to write stories.

She went to Spelman College (for black women) in Atlanta, Georgia, in 1961, transferring to Sarah Lawrence College, New York, in 1963. Here she read widely in many literatures, and took her degree in 1965. She won a writing scholarship for the following year, and in the next two decades held a series of fellowships, awards and teaching appointments, including posts at Wellesley College and Yale University. She married Melvyn R. Levanthal, a (white) Civil Rights lawyer, in 1967; their daughter Rebecca was born in 1969; they were divorced in 1976.

She was a prolific and successful writer from an early age. Her essay 'The Civil Rights Movement: What Good Was It?' won a prize offered by the *American Scholar* in 1967. Her first short story, 'To Hell With Dying', was also published in 1967. *Once: Poems* (1968) was followed by several other collections of her verse. Her first novel, *The Third Life of Grange Copeland*, appeared in 1970. *In Love and Trouble: Stories of Black Women* (1973) and *You Can't Keep A Good Woman Down* (1981) are collections of her short stories. Her critical studies include *Langston Hughes: American Poet* (1974).

Alice Walker was an activist in the Civil Rights Movement which fought to end segregation and to guarantee voting rights for black Americans. Her second novel, *Meridian* (1976), reflects this concern: its heroine works for the rights of poor blacks in the Deep South. Other strong commitments have influenced her work. Her love and concern for Africa, to be seen in her poems, and her passionate feminist beliefs, inspired her novel *The Color Purple* (1982). She prefers the term 'womanist' to 'feminist', and sets out her creed of 'womanism' at the front of her book of essays, *In Search of Our Mothers' Gardens: Womanist Prose* (1983). The first definition of 'womanist' is 'a black feminist', derived from 'womanish' meaning like a woman, as in the black folk saying, 'You acting womanish'. The second sense of the word refers to women who love other women as well as men, prefer women's culture and are devoted to 'the survival and wholeness of their entire people, male and female'. The third sense is of a woman who loves the Spirit, music, culture, struggle and herself; and the fourth declares that 'Womanist is to feminist as purple is to lavender'. This creed is to be seen in all Alice Walker's life and work, including her novel *The Temple of My Familiar* (1989).

It is for *The Color Purple* that Alice Walker is best known. This novel won the American Book Award and the Pulitzer Prize – never before awarded to a black woman. It remained on the *New York Times* best-seller list for more than twenty-five weeks. The film version of the novel, directed by Steven Spielberg (1985), was a huge success. The book also aroused controversy because of its uncompromising portrayal of violence and its sympathetic treatment of sexual love between women. It won the admiration of many readers, not only dedicated feminists, by the warmth and sharpness with which its author wrote about life.

General background

The general background to *The Color Purple* is the history of black people, especially women, in the southern United States in the period between the later nineteenth century and the Second World War, and in Africa during the same (colonial) period.

Alice Walker has argued that the history of black women in modern America should be seen in three stages: the first, ending in the 1930s, and the second, ending in the 1950s, can be seen in *The Color Purple*; the third period corresponds to Walker's adult lifetime. (See the interviews reported by M. H. Washington, *Black American Literature Forum*, vol. 11, 1977, pp. 22–4.)

She calls the first period a time of 'Suspended' life for women, because they were lost in a period that offered no hope of progress. It began with the aftermath of the Civil War. When the Union of the Northern states, under President Abraham Lincoln (1809–65), defeated the Confederacy of Southern states in 1865, slavery was abolished throughout the United States by the 13th Amendment to the Constitution, ratified in December 1865. The 14th Amendment of the following year granted citizenship and equal civil rights to the four million ex-slaves. The 15th Amendment reinforced the right of all Americans to vote, in 1870. Northerners felt satisfied with these measures, and did not closely concern themselves with what actually took place in the South. The economy and social order of the former slave-states had been shattered by the war. Although black people were free, they were still poor, and easy targets for injustice. Their actual right to hold property was precarious; they had little hope of redress when it was taken from them. The father of Celie and Nettie in *The Color Purple* is lynched because his business becomes a threat to his white rivals. The condition of women was little changed. They laboured in the fields as before, and were, in a phrase of the black woman novelist Zora Neale Hurston (1901?–60) that Walker often quotes, 'the mules of the world', laden with every sort of social burden. The reader is shown how these women toiled, insulted and abused by men, black and white, in *The Third Life of Grange Copeland* and in *The Color Purple*. Alice Walker has been particularly concerned to emphasise the stifling of creative talent in the women of this unhappy era.

The women of Alice Walker's second historical phase are said to have been 'assimilated', during the 1940s and 1950s, 'into the mainstream of American life'. This brought a danger of separation from their ethnic background. In the closing stages of *The Color Purple*, the principal female characters, Celie, Shug, Sofia and Mary Agnes, are free from the 'suspended' condition of drudgery in which they were all born at the end of the nineteenth century, and are prospering as professional singers and businesswomen in the early 1940s. The positive side of their achievement is highlighted in this novel, but we see signs of difficulty in race relations in Sofia's troubled dealings with the white woman Eleanor Jane.

Walker's third phase, a time of 'emergent' women, began with the Civil Rights Movement of the 1960s, although thoroughly liberated women belonging to earlier periods appear in her novels; we might consider Shug Avery in *The Color Purple* to be one of them. The novelist herself certainly corresponds to her own definition of a woman of this latest age, 'called to life' by the struggles of the 1960s to fight segregation on buses and in restaurants and to achieve full equality for black citizens. The essays of *In Search of Our Mothers' Gardens* include a tribute to Dr Martin Luther King (1929–68), the great orator and moral leader of the Movement. Walker emphasises in many essays that the Movement changed human attitudes in the American South. The outlook of her mother, who brought up eight children of her own and lots more besides, and believed that black people were inferior to white, belongs to the 'Suspended' era of the past (*In Search of Our Mothers' Gardens*, p. 123).

The Women's Movement is the other modern movement that has deeply influenced Alice Walker, and it has become her foremost commitment. Her loyalties were divided when she was obliged to criticise sexism among fellow Civil Rights activists. Her second novel, *Meridian*, depicts a highly principled young woman, working in the Civil Rights Movement, who adopts a peaceful but feminist programme in place of the masculine goal of violent revolution. By the time she wrote *The Color Purple*, Walker had decided that she must risk male hostility by an unswerving commitment to the plight of black women abused by men of their own race.

The African setting of the novel is less precisely located than the scenes in Georgia and Tennessee. The heroine's sister Nettie is a missionary in West Africa between about 1914 and about 1941. Most of the continent was then under colonial rule. We hear of the Belgian Congo and of Senegal, where the boat taking Nettie out from England makes a stop at the then French-colonial capital, Dakar. Her next stop is in Liberia, which was an independent state created in the nineteenth century as a refuge for black immigrants returning to Africa from the United States. Rubber planting in the territory of the Olinka people, among whom Nettie works in the novel, suggests a setting in Liberia, where rubber was extensively introduced in the 1920s. But Nettie has sailed on from Liberia and seems, from the stamps on her letters and other indications, to be in a British colony. The ruthless character of the road-building and rubber-planting which destroy the homes, fields and way of life of the Olinka are clearly intended to show the treatment of African peoples under colonialism throughout the continent, and not merely one particular case of bad administration. The conservative attitudes of the Olinka men towards the education and emancipation of women, condemned in the novel, are also meant to typify this form of backwardness, which the Africa of the time shared with America.

Religious practice and beliefs are another feature of the background. Protestant Christianity was quickly absorbed into the culture brought to America from Africa during the era of slavery (from the seventeenth to the nineteenth century). Fostered by songs, music and passionate preaching, the Christian faith remained strong among black people after Emancipation. The appeal of 'the black church' to its women can be seen in *The Third Life of Grange Copeland* and in *Meridian*. It has been suggested that Southern Baptist sermons may have influenced Walker's choice of the form of letters to God for her third novel, since it was common for preachers to tell of their talks with the Lord, and Celie would have heard them.

Most of the novel is set in the golden age of jazz and blues singing. 'Duke' Ellington (1899–1974) and Bessie Smith (1894–1937) are among the great artists and entertainers mentioned. The great jazz and blues singers of the time managed to reflect the real stories of ordinary life in their songs. Furthermore, the independent, flamboyant lives of these women were in stark contrast to those of women like Celie. In the character of Shug Avery, we see a reflection of their flair and creative spirit.

Literary background

Alice Walker is among the best known and most admired of the many black women novelists from the South of the United States whose work has been published during the last twenty years. (Other authors and works are included in Part 5, Suggestions for Further reading.) Earlier writers who influenced this new school of novelists, and Alice Walker in particular, are Zora Neale Hurston, whose novel *Their Eyes Were Watching*

God first appeared in 1937, and Margaret Walker (*b.* 1915), author of the epic novel of black American life, *Jubilee* (1966). Walker calls Zora Neale Hurston (whom she has written about and edited) her 'literary progenitor'. She admires Hurston's 'complete, undiminished sense of self'. She has aimed to imitate Hurston's ability 'to let her characters be themselves, funny talk and all', and she admires the way that Hurston was 'incapable of being embarrassed by anything black people did, and so was able to write about everything' (*In Search of Our Mothers' Gardens*, p. 259).

Among other black American writers who have influenced her work, she mentions with special praise Jean Toomer (1894–1967), poet, playwright and fiction-writer, whose novel *Cane* (1923) was a major work of the movement called the Harlem Renaissance; and the poet, songwriter, play-wright, novelist and musician Langston Hughes (1902–67), whom Toomer influenced, and about whom Walker has written a book. She notes of Toomer that 'he has a very feminine sensibility', adding 'unlike most black male writers' (*In Search of Our Mothers' Gardens*, p. 259).

Alice Walker has acknowledged the influence of many writers in other traditions. Among white women writers she admires are the Brontë sisters, Anne (1820–49), Charlotte (1816–55) and Emily (1818–48); Doris Lessing (*b.* 1919), whose work draws on her upbringing in Zimbabwe (then Southern Rhodesia), and whose novel *The Golden Notebook* (1962) treats themes from feminist points of view; and Simone de Beauvoir (1908–86), the French novelist and essayist, author of a key feminist work, translated as *The Second Sex* (*Le deuxième sexe*, 1949). She says of this group of writers that 'well aware of their own oppression', they use their gifts as creative writers to fulfil themselves as women (*In Search of Our Mothers' Gardens*, p. 251)

As a student, Walker read all the Russian novels she could. She learned from Leo Tolstoy (1828–1910) 'to drive through' political and social issues to reach the individual spirit, an effort needed to make characters live (*In Search of Our Mothers' Gardens*, p. 257). She admired the other great Russians of the nineteenth century, but was disappointed to find no Russian women novelists. Among poets, she enjoyed the Americans Emily Dickinson (1830–86) and E. E. Cummings (1894–1962), and the British poet Robert Graves (1895–1985), champion of the White (Moon) Goddess, who represents the creative female principle, long suppressed by male rationalising (*In Search of Our Mothers' Gardens*, p. 257). *The Temple of My Familiar* is dedicated 'To Robert, in whom the Goddess shines'. She also speaks of her enjoyment of the 'sensual' Latin poems of Catullus (*c.* 84–*c.* 54BC) and Ovid (43BC–AD17), and of Japanese *haiku* poets who taught her the possibilities of short forms.

Among African writers, she praises the Nigerian, Elechi Amadi (*b.* 1934), whose novel *The Concubine* (1966) may have influenced her story 'Roselily', a prototype of *The Color Purple*, and the distinguished

South African novelist Bessie Head (1937–86), whose conviction that God is known in Africa in ways undreamt of by missionaries may have influenced the presentation of religious themes in Walker's fiction.

The Color Purple belongs to the genre of epistolary novels. The greatest writer in this tradition was one of the earliest, Samuel Richardson (1689–1761). The novel in letters appealed to women novelists, including Mrs Aphra Behn (1640–89) and Fanny Burney (1752–1840). Jane Austen (1775–1817) also experimented with novels in the form of letters. There have been novels of this kind in the modern period, but the invention of the telephone seems to have impaired the already somewhat restricted nature of the genre. Alice Walker may have had in mind her predecessors among female novelists, but she may also have intended to remind us of Richardson's vast and enthralling novels *Pamela* (1740–1) and *Clarissa* (1747–8), which deal with the plight of women insulted and abused by villainous men. Like Jean Toomer, Richardson was a man with a strong and delicate sensibility.

A note on the text

The Color Purple was published in the United States by Harcourt Brace Jovanovich, New York, 1982. It was published in Great Britain by The Women's Press, London, 1983. These Notes are based on the text of the British edition. The letters are not numbered in any edition of the novel. Students numbering the letters 1–90 for use with these Notes (and other commentaries) must remember that each letter begins on a fresh page. Letters quoted within letters are not to be numbered.

Part 2

Summaries
of THE COLOR PURPLE

A general summary

The story begins in the first decade of the twentieth century. The setting is rural Georgia, and the characters are black Americans. Celie (who is never given a surname) is fourteen years old. Her mother is mentally disturbed. We find out later that this is due to the death of her father, lynched twelve years ago by white business rivals. Celie thinks that her mother's second husband, Alphonso, is her father. She has a younger, much loved sister, Nettie, and numerous small half-brothers and sisters. When Alphonso rapes her she writes a letter to God, asking for a 'sign', because she cannot understand what has happened. This begins a sequence of fifty-one letters from Celie to God, written at intervals over a period of more than thirty years.

Celie's mother dies. Alphonso takes away the two children, a girl and a boy, that Celie bears him. He threatens to rape Nettie, but Celie intervenes, offering herself in her sister's place. When Celie is about nineteen, Alphonso marries her to a local farmer. Celie calls her husband Mr. —— (although his real name is Albert). Her husband treats her brutally, often beating her, and she works in his house and on his farm almost as a slave. One day she sees her daughter, now aged six, and the woman who, with her clergyman-husband, has adopted the child, who is called Olivia. Nettie comes to live with Celie but is soon obliged to flee from the advances of Mr. ——. Celie advises Nettie to seek out the couple who have adopted Olivia.

Mr. —— has four children by his former wife and Celie cares for them. The eldest boy, Harpo, grows up and marries Sofia, a strong, independent-minded woman who loves, but refuses to live in subjection to, her husband. She retaliates very effectively when Harpo tries to beat her. Celie is at first envious of Sofia's free spirit, but they are reconciled after a quarrel and become friends.

Celie and Mr. —— have one thing in common: both are infatuated with the famous singer Shug Avery. Mr. —— has been Shug's lover, and they have had children together. Celie has only seen her in a photograph. When Shug falls ill, Mr. —— takes her in and Celie nurses her. Celie is sexually attracted by Shug and devoted to her, and through her devotion they become friends. Shug calls Mr. —— Albert, and Celie realises that she had forgotten his first name. Sofia has wearied of Harpo's bullying, and moves to one of her sister's with their five children. Harpo converts the house into a jukejoint: a bar with music and dancing. Shug sings there, dedicating a song to 'Miss Celie'.

Sofia returns one evening to the jukejoint. She quarrels with Harpo's girlfriend, Mary Agnes, nicknamed Squeak, and knocks her down. A few days later she quarrels with the wife of the white mayor and, when he strikes her, Sofia knocks him down. She is arrested, badly beaten and sentenced to twelve years' imprisonment. After three years she is placed in the mayor's household as a prisoner-maid to his wife Miss Millie. Shug leaves Celie and Albert, and tours the country as a singer, growing famous and rich.

Years go by. One Christmas, Shug returns with a husband, a toothy, vulgar man called Grady. When Grady and Albert stay out all night drinking, Shug and Celie share a bed, for warmth. Celie tells of how Alphonso abused her. Shug comforts her and they make love.

Shug discovers that Nettie has been writing to her sister for more than twenty years and that Albert has been hiding the letters. She and Celie find bundles of letters in a trunk. A sequence of these letters to Celie now tells us what has become of Nettie. The preacher, Samuel, and his wife Corrine, the couple who adopted Olivia and Celie's other child Adam, have taken Nettie into their household, and she has gone with them as a missionary to Africa. She describes conditions among the Olinka tribe where they have lived and worked ever since. The Olinka are a poor but independent people . until the building of a road and the introduction of rubber plantations, to benefit far-away foreign interests, destroys their way of life.

Corrine notices how closely the children resemble Nettie and is jealous, supposing Nettie to have been Samuel's lover. She accepts the truth only on her deathbed. Nettie now learns that Samuel was formerly acquainted with Alphonso, and knows the facts about the sisters' parentage. Nettie and Samuel go to England to try and help the Olinka, and there they marry. Unfortunately, their efforts on behalf of the Olinka are unsuccessful, and they return disappointed. Adam falls in love with an African girl called Tashi, and becomes distressed because she has her face scarred in a traditional ceremony. Missionary work becomes unfeasible in this part of Africa, and the family hope to return to America.

Nettie's letters are interspersed with letters Celie writes to her. Celie is overjoyed to find that Alphonso is not their father. Shug talks to Celie about religion, and persuades her that God is not to be pictured as a wise old (white) man, but worshipped as a power in Nature and a spiritual force within us. Sofia is released from service in the mayor's house. Mary Agnes becomes a professional singer. She goes off to Panama with Grady, and Sofia returns to Harpo. Celie announces that she means to leave Albert and go to live with Shug in Memphis. She curses her husband and he denounces her as a poor, ugly, black woman, that is to say 'nothing at all'.

Celie proves him wrong when she goes to Memphis, where she runs a successful business called 'Folkspants, Unlimited', and lives happily with Shug. It is Albert who goes into a decline, having to be nursed back to health by Harpo. He only recovers when he returns the remainder of Nettie's letters to Celie, and is thus freed from his wife's curse.

Alphonso dies. Celie and Nettie inherit land and a business, formerly their father's and willed to them, but withheld by Alphonso. Celie is heart-broken when Shug falls for Germaine, a young man in her band, and tours the country with her new boyfriend. Sofia's sixth child (not Harpo's), Henrietta, becomes sick, and Celie nurses her. There is a false report of Nettie's death in the Atlantic (by this time the Second World War has started). Shug leaves Germaine and returns to Celie. Albert is now a reformed character; he has even taken up sewing. He and Celie have friendly talks; she even mentions his name, but there is no chance of a revival of their marriage. Celie tells him frankly that she has always found men physically unappealing.

The last letter sees the reconciliation of all the principal characters. Nettie and Samuel, Adam and his wife Tashi, with Olivia, come safely home, and Celie has a family at last. This, the ninetieth letter, is addressed to 'Dear God, Dear stars, dear trees, dear sky, dear peoples. Dear Everything', and offers thanks for happiness at last.

Detailed summaries

Letter 1

A fourteen-year-old girl is writing to God because she has no one else to confide in. She does not give her name; we learn in Letter 7 that she is called Celie. Celie has been raped by a man called Alphonso ('Fonso'), apparently living with her mother. We learn in Letter 6 that Celie believes the man to be her father. (He eventually turns out to be her stepfather.) The girl describes what happened in blunt but innocent terms. It is obvious that she does not understand that she has been raped, but feels very distressed nonetheless. She hopes that God will send her 'a sign'.

NOTES AND GLOSSARY:
You better not ... mammy: we assume these to be the words of her 'father', Alphonso
Lucious: Lucius
fussing: quarrelling
too soon: too soon after the birth of her last child
Naw, I ain't gonna: no, I am not going to
Macon: a city in Georgia
kine: kind

Letter 2

More than a year must have passed, because Celie is pregnant for the second time. The birth of the first baby astonished Celie. When her mother asked who was responsible, she said that God was. Alphonso took the baby away and, she believes (wrongly, as we find out in Letter 10), killed it in the woods. Celie told her mother that 'God took it'. Her mother has since died, in agony and rage, and it seems that Alphonso felt some genuine grief at her death. Celie tells God that she fears Alphonso will kill her next baby too. Meanwhile she has to keep house, and act as nanny to all her smaller brothers and sisters.

NOTES AND GLOSSARY:

cussing:	swearing
big:	pregnant
set:	sat
bout:	about
ast:	asked

Letter 3

More months have passed. Alphonso has not killed Celie's second baby, but sold it to a childless couple living some distance away. Alphonso tells her she is 'evil', disobedient and 'indecent' because she has milk running down her body and no proper clothes. He does nothing to help her. She hopes he will marry again soon. He is looking lustfully at Nettie, Celie's younger sister. Nettie is afraid, but Celie means to protect her, God willing.

NOTES AND GLOSSARY:

Monticello:	a town in Georgia
fine:	find

Letter 4

Celie is reluctant to give Alphonso a name, usually writing only 'he', but in this letter she calls him 'Pa'. Pa has brought home a new wife, a teenage girl of about Celie's age. This girl seems to like her husband, but is bewildered by her new duties in a house with so many young children. A widower with three children is interested in Nettie, and he visits her every Sunday. Celie calls him Mr. ——. His wife was killed 'by her boyfriend coming home from church'. Celie is sure that Nettie will do better to continue attending classes at the local school, rather than submit to such a marriage.

NOTES AND GLOSSARY:
Gray: a town in Georgia
boyfriend: suitor
in the same shape: of the same age and build
more than a notion: a serious undertaking
ain't even yourn: are not even yours

Letter 5

Alphonso has beaten Celie, she reports to God, for winking at a boy in church. She did not wink, and she does not look at men. She looks at women instead. She finds women more attractive because they do not frighten her. She mentions that God might be surprised at this, as her mother swore at her. She denies that she feels angry with her mother, blaming her Pa's lies for her mother's death. When she sees Pa looking at Nettie, she stands in his way. She advises Nettie to marry her admirer, because that will save her from Pa. She says that Nettie may be able to enjoy one more year of her youth before the pregnancies begin. Celie does not expect to become pregnant again.

NOTES AND GLOSSARY:
cause: because
cuss me: swore at me
mad: angry
story: lies

Letter 6

Mr. —— asks Alphonso for Nettie's 'hand in marriage'. Alphonso refuses on the grounds that Nettie is too young and Mr. —— has too many children. His last wife, furthermore, died in scandalous circumstances. There are further scandalous rumours about a liaison between Mr. —— and a woman called Shug Avery.

Shug Avery interests Celie and her 'new mammy', who manages to obtain a picture. Shug turns out to be a beautiful woman, rouged and dressed in furs, with a certain sadness about the eyes. The photograph shows her in front of a motor-car. Celie is fascinated by this romantic image. She stares at the photograph every night, and dreams about Shug – 'dressed to kill', and dancing and laughing.

NOTES AND GLOSSARY:
ast: asked
billfold: wallet
somethin tail: animal fur

Letter 7

We learn Celie's name, and that she is now nearly twenty. While her new mother is sick, Celie has to protect Nettie from Pa by offering herself instead. To make herself more alluring, she dresses herself up as well as she can. She succeeds in rescuing her sister, although she also suffers another beating and sexual assault for her effrontery.

Mr. —— calls again, terrifying Nettie. Alphonso, however, refuses to part with Nettie, saying that he means to make a schoolteacher of her when she has had some more education. In her place he offers Celie. He talks about her as though he were selling a slave. He tells Mr. —— that although she is ugly and not a virgin, Celie has two advantages: she works hard, and she is not able to bear any more children. Obliged to listen to this account of herself, Celie finds consolation in gazing into the sad but powerful eyes of Shug Avery in the treasured picture. Alphonso offers to give Celie a dowry: her own linen and a cow. Mr. —— is left to consider this handsome offer.

NOTES AND GLOSSARY:

horsehair:	worn as a hair-piece
trampy:	behaving like a prostitute
Sides:	besides
ain't fresh:	is not a virgin
spect:	expect
God done fixed her:	it is believed that she is now infertile
it *bees*:	it is. Shug's eyes seem to say that insults from men are an inevitable part of life
crib:	barn

Letter 8

Spring has gone by, and Mr. —— has decided to marry Celie. She thinks only of Nettie, whom she hopes to be able to save from Alphonso. Perhaps this will be easier, she tells herself, when she is married to Mr. —— since he obviously still prefers Nettie. The sisters may be able to run away together. Meanwhile they are working hard at Nettie's schoolbooks, trying to make themselves well enough educated to survive in the world on their own if they do run away. Celie has not been to school since the time of her first pregnancy (five years ago), since her love of school meant nothing to her Pa. He ignored the pleas of Nettie, whom he thought the cleverer, and those of the teacher, Miss Beasley, whom he scorned as a garrulous spinster. Miss Beasley tried to intervene on Celie's behalf, but gave up when she saw that Celie was pregnant.

Mr. —— comes to make a final inspection of Celie. She has to turn about before him while he sits on his horse and Alphonso reads his newspaper. Mr. —— agrees to take Celie as his wife only when he is reassured that the cow is still included in the bargain.

NOTES AND GLOSSARY:

Columbus ... Santomareater: Christopher Columbus (1451–1506) sailed from Spain in 1492 with three ships: the *Santa Maria*, the *Pinta* and the *Niña*

Indians ... queen: Columbus took slaves back from the New World as one of his gifts for King Ferdinand V and Queen Isabella of Spain, who had financed his voyage

run off at the mouth: talks too much

bout the ground ... flat: that the earth is a sphere

how flat it look to me: just the way it looks; the meaning behind this is that life seems so unpromising to Celie

drug out: exhausted

Like it wasn't nothing: as though it were an unimportant matter

nary one of them: not one of the children

Letter 9

Celie is married. On her wedding night Mr. ——'s eldest boy, a twelve-year-old, throws a stone which cuts her head. His mother died in his arms, and he wants no stepmother. It turns out that Mr. —— has four children, all hard work to look after. Celie lies in bed with Mr. ——, thinking about how to keep Nettie safe. Then she thinks about Shug Avery, who perhaps used to enjoy what Mr. —— is now doing to her. This thought makes her put an arm around her husband.

NOTES AND GLOSSARY:

died in his arms: the child's mother was killed by her boyfriend after church, as we learn in Letter 4

cuse: accuse

Letter 10

Celie sees a little girl bearing a strong resemblance to herself and to Alphonso, walking in town behind the woman who has adopted her (or bought her). She is about the right age to be the baby taken from Celie six years ago. Celie's heart tells her that this is her first child, whom she named Olivia.

Olivia's new mother is buying cloth in the store. Celie approaches and finds out that the new father is a clergyman. The storekeeper speaks contemptuously to both women (in a manner that suggests he must be white) and they leave. Since the Reverend Mr. —— has not yet arrived, they sit in Celie's husband's wagon to wait. As they talk we learn for the first time that Celie's husband is a notably handsome man. She admits that men all look alike to her. Her daughter's adoptive parents have named the little girl Pauline, but given her the pet name of Olivia. The Reverend Mr. —— makes a brief appearance, a large man. Olivia's new mother has a lively sense of fun. When Mr. —— returns, he finds to his annoyance that Celie is bursting with laughter.

NOTES AND GLOSSARY:

long hind:	along behind
embroder:	embroider
daidies:	nappies
long side:	along the side of
bidniss:	business
clerk:	shop assistant
Girl:	a contemptuous form of address to a black woman. See Letter 71 for a comment on the offence this incident causes
bolt:	a large roll of cloth, straight from the loom
tare:	tore
thout:	without
clam:	climbs
don't hit on much:	don't look smart
nuff:	enough
ole:	old
git it:	understand (the word-play on 'hospitality')

Letter 11

Nettie comes to stay with Celie and her husband, having run away from Alphonso. Her presence is a comfort to Celie, to whom she passes on what she has learned at school. Nettie urges Celie to control the children with a firmer hand, and to try to fight in the battle of life; Celie says she only knows how to survive. She still cares more about Nettie than about herself, and is afraid that her sister's talents will be lost if she has to marry a man like Mr. ——.

Mr. —— has agreed to let Nettie stay because he hopes to seduce her. When she resists his advances, he says she must leave. There is an emotional parting. Celie advises her to seek the help of the Reverend Mr. ——'s wife – the only woman Celie has ever seen allowed to handle money for herself. Celie says she will not be alone so long as she can spell G-o-d. They agree to write to each other. But after Nettie has gone, no letters arrive.

NOTES AND GLOSSARY:
they mean: they are inconsiderate
tention: attention
teefs: teeth
to make miration over: to make a fuss about showing admiration
us done help Nettie: we have helped Nettie
Stead: instead
is all: is her only regret
mine: mind
along: with me

Letter 12

Carrie and Kate, two of Mr. —'s sisters, come to stay. They praise Celie's housekeeping warmly, stressing this as a duty of all married women, sadly neglected by Mr. —'s previous wife, Annie Julia. She had not wanted to marry Mr. — at all; once married, he continued his pursuit of his former lover, Shug Avery, with no regard for his wife's feelings. Celie is a wife to be valued: tireless in keeping house, cooking and tending the children.

Kate comes again, this time alone, and urges her brother to buy his wife some clothes, instead of keeping her in rags. When Kate takes her to buy the clothes, Celie day-dreams about Shug Avery. She considers what colour of dress Shug Avery would wear. Shug is like a queen to Celie, and so she thinks it would be purple, the royal colour, with maybe a little red to brighten it. But Mr. — is unlikely to waste his money on such expensive colours, so Celie settles for blue, and is overcome with the dress – the first that has ever been made for her.

Kate tells the eldest boy, Harpo, to help Celie with the chores. Harpo refuses, saying that such work is only fit for women. When Kate insists, Harpo tells Mr. —, who sends her home. Kate offers Celie the advice she has already received from Nettie: she should learn to fight for herself. Celie says nothing, but thinks that by doing as she is told, at least she will stay alive. Nettie tried to fight, and now (so Celie thinks) she is dead.

NOTES AND GLOSSARY:
a nasty 'oman bout the house: a poor housekeeper
spose: is supposed
direar: diarrhoea
newmonya: pneumonia
It need: does she need
a trifling nigger: a silly boy. The novel is historically accurate in attributing 'nigger', and other now unacceptable terms, to black as well as white speakers

Letter 13

Harpo is curious to hear about how wives are best managed, and asks his father, who tells him they must be beaten, especially when they are as stubborn as Celie. Celie tries to make herself wooden, like a tree. This, she says, is how she knows that 'trees fear man'. Harpo tells Celie that he is in love with a girl. He has only winked at her in church, but he tells Celie that they plan to marry, although he is only seventeen, and she fifteen, and he has not yet spoken to her. This may be why he has asked his father's advice about wives.

NOTES AND GLOSSARY:
bug: round
yall: you (plural)
Amen corner: at prayer

Letter 14

Shug Avery is coming to town to sing at the Lucky Star saloon. Celie and her husband are both highly excited. Mr. —— dresses carefully, for once. Pink posters, picturing Shug as 'Queen Honeybee', are fastened to trees. Celie has no hope of being allowed to attend a performance, but would love a chance to see Shug.

NOTES AND GLOSSARY:
orkestra: a blues band
pomade: hair oil
hanksters: handkerchiefs
hick: country bumpkin
like Indian Chiefs: covered with feathers
Queen Honeybee: because she is sweet; 'Shug' is an abbreviation of Sugar

Letter 15

Mr. —— spends the weekend in town, returning tired and sad. Celie longs to question him about Shug. She works long hours in the field chopping cotton, unaided by Mr. ——, who makes a feeble attempt to help before returning to the verandah to smoke his pipe and stare into space.

NOTES AND GLOSSARY:
Where you all children at . . .?: where are your and Shug's children . . .?
Feel like snakes: evil thoughts
porch: a broad verandah

Letter 16

The love-sick Mr. —— now sits hopelessly all day, staring at nothing. Harpo, afraid of his father, is obliged to do all the ploughing. Wife and son labour like slaves. Celie thinks that Harpo's weakness makes him look womanly. Harpo is still in love.

Letter 17

Harpo's girl's father rejects him as a suitor because his mother's murder is still reckoned a disgrace. Harpo suffers nightmares, reliving the scene of his mother's death. The 'boyfriend' shot her in the stomach and she died in his arms. Waking in the night, Harpo trembles and protests to Celie that his mother was not to blame.

Celie is kind to Mr. ——'s children, but has no affection, or any other feeling about them. Harpo continues to confide in her, however, praising the beauty of his girl, whom he now names as Sofia. He hopes that he will be regarded as a more acceptable husband once he has succeeded in making her pregnant. Once she is pregnant, he brings her to visit his father. They come marching up the road, hand in hand, Sofia in front. She is a large, strong girl, intelligent and independent minded, quite unafraid of Mr. ——. She has left home, but is living with her married sister; she tells Mr. —— that she will wait there until Harpo is allowed to marry her. When she leaves, the men of the house are both at a loss what to do or say, because they are unaccustomed to such an outspoken woman.

NOTES AND GLOSSARY:

chifferobe:	wardrobe
Bright:	having light-brown skin
notty:	knotty

Letter 18

Harpo marries Sofia; the baby in her arms is a big 'nursing' boy. He brings them back to a small house on his father's land, which they repair. Harpo begins to receive wages and he works more willingly. Sofia remains a strong, confident girl, and they are happy together. Only Mr. —— is cynical about their future.

NOTES AND GLOSSARY:

goose:	encourage
pot:	pot-belly
mash:	crushed
switch the traces on you:	deceive you with another man

Letter 19

Trouble comes from Harpo's fixed idea that Sofia ought to obey him. She loves him, but has no intention of behaving like the submissive Celie. Mr. —— disapproves. Wives are like children, he says, and must be beaten if they are to be kept in order. Celie thinks that the marriage, now three years old, would be a happy one if Harpo would only forget his father's teaching and accept Sofia as she is. But Celie also resents Sofia's independent ways, and especially dislikes seeing Sofia pity her. When Harpo asks for advice, she tells him to beat Sofia. The next time she sees Harpo, his face is a mass of bruises. He tells unlikely tales about a mule and a barn door. Sofia retains the upper hand.

NOTES AND GLOSSARY:
backtalk: talks back to me
mind: obey
primping: preening, smartening up
Nome: no, ma'am

Letter 20

Harpo and Sofia continue to have fist-fights. Celie witnesses one appalling contest, where they tear their house apart, and which Sofia wins. She and Harpo, with the two babies, leave in the wagon the next day, as she wanted, to visit her married sister.

NOTES AND GLOSSARY:
hants: ghosts
ease on back out: eased my way out

Letter 21

Celie has trouble getting to sleep for over a month and decides that she is suffering for her sin against Sofia. She hopes that Sofia will not find out that she advised Harpo to use violence. Harpo tells, however, and Sofia is furious. Celie confesses that she is jealous of Sofia's ability to fight for herself. Sofia talks about her childhood. She was one of twelve children, six girls and six boys. The girls were obliged to learn to fight, and to stick together. No girl is safe from her own male kin, Sofia says, unless she can fight. Celie says, piously, that life is short, but Heaven will be for ever. Sofia recommends bashing Mr. ——'s head open, and thinking about Heaven later. They collapse in laughter, and then set to work on quilt-making, a sign of female solidarity throughout the novel. Celie can sleep once more.

NOTES AND GLOSSARY:
witch hazel: a herbal remedy for ills
toting: carrying
Bible say ... mother: See the Bible, Deuteronomy 5:16
Old Maker: God

Letter 22

Shug is ill, and everyone has turned against her, except Mr. —— and Celie. The preacher at church and her parents at home have condemned her, but Mr. —— goes off in his wagon and brings her home five days later, sick and stumbling, but still 'dressed to kill'. Celie is fascinated by the 'mean' look on Shug's now feverish face, and by the enigmatic tone of her cackling voice. Her greeting is 'mean': 'You sure *is* ugly'.

NOTES AND GLOSSARY:
Tramp ... strumpet ... hussy: terms for a prostitute
two berkulosis: tuberculosis
Puzzle: she puzzles them
got his mouth on: speaks against
amen: in this novel 'amen' tends to imply mindless religious conformism
mean: American usage has the senses of 'hostile', 'malicious', 'troublesome' and 'hard to defeat'

Letter 23

Shug is sicker than Celie's mother on her deathbed, but she is more 'evil', Celie says, and that keeps her alive. Her strength of will is undiminished. She hectors Mr. ——, whom she calls Albert, even forbidding him to smoke in her sickroom, where he mopes in the shadows. Celie is astonished to see how easily he can be subdued. She had forgotten his name. She notices for the first time that Albert has a weak chin. It is also the first time that he and she share a concern, in their common devotion to Shug. He consults Celie, for once, asking her if she minds having Shug in the house. Although Celie continues to call him Mr. —— until almost the end of the novel, the reader is likely to follow other characters in thinking of him as Albert. He seems less of a monster from now on. He sheds a tear of sympathy for Shug at the end of this letter.

Letter 24

Although Shug and Albert have had three children together, he is uncomfortable about giving her a bath, so Celie has to do it. When Shug is naked for her bath, Celie is so attracted by the sight of her long body that she wonders if she has turned into a man. Her hands tremble as she washes her patient. They begin to talk. Shug rejects Celie's deferential 'ma'am'. She tells Celie she never misses her children, who live with their grandmother.

NOTES AND GLOSSARY:
her mouth . . . claws: she is catty in speech
bat her eyes: flutter her eyelids

Letter 25

Shug refuses food, confining herself to coffee and cigarettes while she looks through fashion magazines, seeming to be puzzled by their images of white women in high society. (These pictures remind us that we are now in the 1920s.) Celie tempts her successfully with the smell of home-cured ham. This puts Celie and Albert in so good a humour that they laugh together. Albert looks slightly crazy because he has been so afraid.

NOTES AND GLOSSARY:
grits: porridge made from ground oats
biscuits: scones
flapjacks: pancakes

Letter 26

Shug begins to get better, tended by the attentive, loving Celie. She treats Shug with the care she would like to show her daughter Olivia. Shug composes a song inspired, she says, by Celie.

NOTES AND GLOSSARY:
a rat to pomp: a pad of hair to fluff out the wearer's own hair
she melt down: she relaxes
scratch out my head: draw from my mind

Letter 27

Albert's father arrives; a small, pompous and indignant man. While he denounces Shug, Celie spits in his glass of water and wonders how to prepare ground glass. The incident brings Albert and Celie closer than ever before, in shared hostility to the old man and loyalty to Shug. Albert's brother Tobias is the next visitor. He brings a ridiculously small box of chocolates and a large amount of vulgar curiosity. Celie teaches Shug to sew quilts. Sitting between Shug and Albert, united with them in opposition to Tobias and all the outside world, she feels happy.

NOTES AND GLOSSARY:

shet:	shut
nappy:	fuzzy
a right smart:	a large part
cornrowed:	done in small plaits
fly speck:	very small

Letter 28

Sofia and Celie work on a quilt. Sofia is worried about Harpo, who has become absurdly gluttonous, consuming vast amounts of fattening food. Harpo likes housework and Sofia likes working outdoors, so they ought to get on well together, but Harpo is obviously unhappy about something. He gorges between meals, and, the women agree, has started to look pregnant. Celie watches him with growing concern.

NOTES AND GLOSSARY:

You feeling yourself:	Sofia thinks Celie is talking nonsense
clabber:	curds
troth:	trough (spelt as she pronounces it)

Letter 29

Harpo breaks down in tears one night while staying with Albert and Celie. He tells Celie how much he wants Sofia to obey him, or at least pay some attention to what he tells her. Sofia refuses to 'mind' him, and she blacks his eyes when he tries to beat her. Celie urges him to accept Sofia as she is, a good wife who loves him. Harpo seems unable to take this advice.

NOTES AND GLOSSARY:

clam round:	climbed around, searched
she tickle:	she amuses
retard:	retarded

Letter 30

Celie visits Sofia. It seems that Harpo is overeating because he hopes to match his wife's weight and improve his chances in their presently un-equal combats. But Sofia is weary of Harpo's obsession with power: he wants a dog, not a wife, she says. She intends to take the children and move to her sister's home. Celie is shocked, but also filled with envy at the idea of having such a refuge. Sofia still loves her husband but their sexual relations are now cold and unfulfilling. All that she really wants is a change of scene for a while.

NOTES AND GLOSSARY:
shingles: thin oblong pieces of roofing material
like running ... on itself: her love for another woman seems to lead nowhere

Letter 31

Sofia's sisters arrive in strength to escort her. Celie presents her with the finished quilt. Powerless to stop his wife's departure, Harpo is a sorry sight as he says goodbye to his children, changing the baby for the last time and drying his tears on the nappy.

NOTES AND GLOSSARY:
seining: netting
Dilsey, Coco and Boo: the names of their cows

Letter 32

Six months have passed since Sofia left. Harpo is greatly changed. Having been thoroughly domesticated as a husband, he is now determined to make money and is converting his house into a jukejoint where his friend Swain will play jazz and people will come out from town for dancing and entertainment. He seems sure Sofia will not return.

NOTES AND GLOSSARY:
shut up the racket: stop the noise
jukejoint: a bar and dance-hall; placed out of easy reach of the police because of Prohibition

Letter 33

In the first few weeks nobody comes to Harpo's jukejoint, apart from friendly visits by Albert and Shug. Then Harpo recruits Shug as a singer. Posters go back on the trees. The bar is filled to overcrowding on Saturday nights. Celie is not allowed to go to such a disreputable kind of establishment; she longs in vain to hear Shug sing. Then Albert's objections are overruled by Shug herself, and Celie goes to a performance. She suffers from jealousy because Shug seems to have eyes only for Albert. Then Shug sings Miss Celie's song – the one Celie helped her scratch out of her head. Nobody has ever dedicated a song to her before, and she has never felt so proud.

NOTES AND GLOSSARY:
box: guitar

chitlins:	chitterlings, fried pork intestines
shifts:	dresses
Bessie Smith:	(1894–1937) a brilliant entertainer and singer; known as 'the Empress of the Blues', she was immensely successful in the 1920s. The American dramatist Edward Albee (*b.* 1928) based his play, *The Death of Bessie Smith* (1960), on the (groundless) popular belief that her life might have been saved after her fatal motor accident if a hospital for whites had admitted her
sassy:	cheeky

Letter 34

Shug sings every weekend at Harpo's place and they both make good money. Singing restores Shug to full health and she decides to leave. When she hears Celie's fear that Albert will start beating her again once she has gone, she promises to stay until she can be sure that he will not do it.

NOTES AND GLOSSARY:
smart money: good money
lightening bugs: fireflies

Letter 35

Celie is jealous because Shug is now sleeping with Albert. When she discusses this with Shug, she conceals the fact that it is Shug, not Albert, she wants to keep for herself. Shug tries to explain her passion for Albert: he is small and amusing and 'smells right'. She is amazed by Celie's confession that she has never enjoyed sexual relations with men. She tells Celie this means she is still a virgin, and begins to teach her about sexual pleasure. Celie still feels jealous at night.

NOTES AND GLOSSARY:
rassle: rustle
not with my sponge and all: this refers to her method of contraception
heist: hoist
prankish: mischievous

Letter 36

Sofia returns. She appears at the jukejoint with Henry Broadnax, known as Buster, a man who looks like a prize-fighter. Sofia and Harpo dance, until Harpo's girlfriend, known as Squeak, quarrels with, and slaps, Sofia. Sofia's tough upbringing has made her return any blow by instinct. She knocks Squeak down, dislodging two teeth.

NOTES AND GLOSSARY:
white lightening: corn whiskey
scandless: scandal
teenouncy: cheeky

Letter 37

Celie advises Squeak to make Harpo call her by her real name, Mary Agnes, because that will make him take her seriously when he is in trouble. Trouble has come: Sofia is in prison. Celie relates to Mary Agnes how Sofia met Miss Millie, the mayor's wife, who made a fuss of her children and then asked if Sofia would care to work as her maid. Appalled at the thought of becoming a white woman's servant, Sophia replied, 'Hell, no'. The mayor slapped Sofia, who knocked him down. Celie cannot go on with the story, so Albert tells how the police beat Sofia before they arrested her, their guns on the prize-fighter. Mary Agnes runs to comfort Harpo. Albert persuades the sheriff to allow a prison visit. Sofia is badly injured and bruised purple all over. Celie attends to her as well as she can.

NOTES AND GLOSSARY:
tension: attention
going on over colored: making a fuss over black people
Just long ... colored: so long as Albert remembers the difference in status between the white sheriff and himself
eggplant: aubergine, coloured purple

Letter 38

The prison visits take place twice a month for half an hour. Sofia works in the prison laundry, in horrible conditions. She learns to behave like Celie, always obedient. But the twelve years of her sentence are 'a long time to be good', as she ruefully jokes. Mary Agnes is helping Sofia's sister Odessa to look after the children.

Letter 39

Celie, Shug, Mary Agnes, Odessa and two more of Sofia's sisters, Albert and the prize-fighter meet to discuss what to do, because they fear for Sofia's sanity. Harpo and the prize-fighter dream of violent steps. Celie dreams of rescue by angels. A practical plan is devised when it is realised that the light-skinned Mary Agnes is related to the white prison-warden, Bubber Hodges. Bubber is her uncle.

Letter 40

Mary Agnes is dressed as a white woman, except that the clothes are patchier. The plan is for her to remind the warden that they are related and that he once gave her a present when she was a child. She must then persuade him that Sofia is quite happy in the laundry, but would loathe being forced to work as a white woman's maid: that would be a real punishment. The idea behind the plan is that the warden will believe that Mary Agnes wishes Sofia harm as she lives with Harpo, and as her kinsman he will fulfil her wish and make Sofia a maid.

NOTES AND GLOSSARY:

look like a quilt: having a chequered design
Uncle Tom: *Uncle Tom's Cabin* (1851–2), by Harriet Elizabeth Beecher Stowe (1811–96), is a novel depicting the miseries of slavery in America. Uncle Tom gave his name to the type of black person who was deferential to whites

Letter 41

The warden is not pleased to be reminded of his kinship with Squeak. He listens to her story, and then asks her to undo her clothing and commits what he calls 'a little fornication'. She goes home with her dress torn. She has suffered in a good cause, however, and has acquired a new self-confidence, in spite of humiliation. When Harpo says he loves her, she demands her rightful name, not Squeak but Mary Agnes.

NOTES AND GLOSSARY:

crackers: an insulting term
Shoot: a mild exclamation of surprise
preshate: appreciate
or just my color: she thinks her light skin her chief attraction

Letter 42

Six months pass, and Mary Agnes becomes a singer. Her small, high voice seems odd after Shug's singing, but she soon becomes popular. She is still angry about the teeth that were knocked out, but she helps to care for Sofia's children all the same.

Letter 43

Three years later, the prison authorities have followed Mary Agnes's suggestion and transferred Sofia from the laundry to duties outside the prison as nursemaid to Miss Millie's children. The mayor's six-year-old son shouts orders, and tries to kick Sofia. She moves out of the way, and the boy hurts his foot. Sofia would be blamed if it were not for the little girl, Eleanor Jane, who dotes on her nurse and testifies to what really happened. Sofia has recovered her physical health, but she broods on violent revenge.

Letter 44

The mayor has bought his wife a new car, but he declines to teach her to drive. Sofia, who used to drive Buster's car, gives Miss Millie lessons. In return, Miss Millie drives Sofia home to spend Christmas Day with her family. She is a well-meaning but ineffectual woman, who does not let Sofia sit beside her in the car because that is not done 'in the South'. As things turn out, Millie's incompetence spoils Sofia's one holiday, and she manages to spend only fifteen minutes with her family.

Letter 45

The story of Celie and Shug is resumed; we can work out later that several years must have passed since the last letter. Shug comes to stay for Christmas and brings a surprise – a new husband. He is a toothy, vulgar man called Grady whom Celie instantly dislikes. She and Albert are extremely jealous. Rich and famous, Shug is driving a new car. She is slow to greet Celie, but does so warmly.

NOTES AND GLOSSARY:
toof: toothy
suspenders: braces

Letter 46

The men drink their way through Christmas, while the women work, talk and celebrate. Shug seems indifferent to the pain she is causing Albert and Celie. Celie confesses that she still is, in Shug's sense, a virgin.

NOTES AND GLOSSARY:
Sophie Tucker: (1884–1966) black American singer, actress and entertainer. Known as 'the Last of the Red Hot Mommas', she sang with great attack, but also had sentimental songs, including 'The Lady is a Tramp'

| Duke Ellington: | Edward Kennedy 'Duke' Ellington (1899–1974), black American band leader; the most influential writer and arranger in the history of jazz. His compositions include 'Mood Indigo' |
| licks: | blows |

Letter 47

Albert and Grady go off in the car and Shug sleeps with Celie for warmth. Celie tells her how she was raped by Alphonso when she was fourteen, and she recalls the horror of those days as she lies in Shug's arms. They make love.

NOTES AND GLOSSARY:
Wellsah: well sir (an exclamation of surprise)

Letter 48

Sleeping with Shug feels like heaven to Celie. It lasts until the men return at dawn, when Albert falls into bed, drunk and snoring. Grady annoys Shug by calling her Mama, and by making eyes at Mary Agnes. Shug is generous to her, however, and encourages her to start a career as a professional singer.

NOTES AND GLOSSARY:
like somebody from the North: attempting to appear sophisticated

Letter 49

Celie has a letter from Nettie at long last. Celie has told Shug about the mystery of Nettie's failure to write. Shug has seen Albert pocketing letters with foreign stamps. We can guess why Nettie's letters have never reached Celie. Nettie's letter shows that she has guessed too: Albert must have been intercepting her letters. She continues to write at Christmas and Easter, just in case one may get through. She says that Olivia and Celie's son are alive and well and coming home soon.

NOTES AND GLOSSARY:
mailbox: on a post by the road, well away from the house
funny stamps: foreign stamps
a little fat white woman: the Queen of England, we learn in the next letter, although the King's head would have appeared on British stamps at any date during the period covered by the novel

Letter 50

Shug has become friendly with Albert again. She walks to the mailbox
with him. This is how she secured Nettie's letter. Celie is so angry about
Albert's theft that she is in danger of cutting his throat until Shug takes
the razor from her. Shug tells Celie about her early life. Her puritanical
mother soon rejected her. She found comfort in loving Albert, who joked
and danced better than anyone when he was young. Shug bore his three
children. When she was finally turned out of the house by her parents, she
went to live with a 'wild' aunt in Memphis, Tennessee. Albert married
Annie Julia because his father insisted that Shug was 'trash' and Albert
was too weak to stand up for himself. Shug regrets her heartless behaviour
to Annie Julia. She is puzzled by Albert's cruelty to Celie.

NOTES AND GLOSSARY:

buddy-buddy:	friendly
reefer:	cannabis
Lillie:	the first mention of her Christian name
roadhouse:	roadside bar and restaurant
the moochie:	the partners in this slow dance stand very close

Letter 51

Celie and Shug find bundles of letters from Nettie in Albert's trunk. They
steam the envelopes open and reclaim the contents, replacing the empty
envelopes in the trunk.

Letter 52

From Nettie to Celie. Nettie urges Celie to leave Albert. She relates how
Albert followed and tried to rape her on the day she fled from his house.
She fought him off. In fury he threatened that neither sister would ever
hear from the other again. Nettie has reached the Reverend Mr. ——'s
house, and found Olivia there.

NOTES AND GLOSSARY:

You've got to fight:	this letter must have been written shortly after Nettie left
some mad:	very angry

Letter 53

From Nettie to Celie. Nettie begs for a letter as soon as possible. The
woman Celie met in the store is called Corrine and her husband is called

Samuel. The little girl is now known as Olivia. There is also a little boy called Adam. The family are very kind to Nettie, involving her in their work for the church.

NOTES AND GLOSSARY:
too soon: this letter must have been written some weeks after Letter 52
Adam: we do not learn that he is Celie's son until Letter 55
sanctified religious: dedicated Christians
the time you laid yourself down: this refers to Celie's offering of herself to save Nettie from Alphonso, as described in Letter 7

Letter 54

From Nettie to Celie. Nettie is very worried about Celie's failure to reply and about her own situation. She is unable to find suitable work. Corrine, Samuel and the children are about to go to Africa as missionaries. She begs for a letter.

Letter 55

From Nettie to Celie. Celie's headnote to this letter tells us that it is dated two months after Letter 54. Nettie is now in Africa. She wrote almost every day of the journey, but destroyed these letters in a moment of despair. Now she has decided to write to Celie in the same desperate hope that made Celie start writing to God. She describes a meeting she had before leaving with a woman who we know from her description must be Sofia (at the time she worked as Miss Millie's nursemaid). She then hears from Samuel and Corrine about how this lady came to be imprisoned. This episode inspired her to accept Samuel's invitation to accompany the family to 'the middle of Africa' as a missionary. She assures Celie that Olivia and Adam are her children and that they are growing up happily.

NOTES AND GLOSSARY:
***two months later*:** this implies that the earlier letters were dated within a shorter space of time. Letter 54 could be months but not years later than Letter 53, which obviously follows soon after Letter 52. Less than a year can have passed since Celie and Nettie parted
her maid: Sofia lives for several years with Harpo and is in prison for three years before working as a maid. See pp. 69–70, in Part 4 below, for an account of the novel's time-scheme

Atlanta:	the state capital of Georgia
Milledgeville:	a town in Georgia

Letter 56

From Nettie to Celie. Nettie feels one of the family rather than a maid; she studies and she teaches the children. She describes her stay in New York before boarding the ship, and praises Harlem, where black people live with dignity and faith. The enthusiastic support and generous fund-raising of church people in Harlem is contrasted with the cold and haughty manners of white people in the Missionary Society.

NOTES AND GLOSSARY:

gored:	formed with wedge-shaped panels of cloth
boater:	a flat straw-hat
Harlem:	the section of New York City between East River and Harlem River at the northern end of Manhattan Island
Speke:	John Hanning Speke (1827–64), British explorer. He discovered and named Lake Victoria, and explored the upper waters of the Nile
Livingstone:	the Reverend Dr David Livingstone (1813–73), British missionary and explorer
Stanley:	Sir Henry Morton Stanley (1841–1904), British explorer and journalist. He was foreign correspondent for the *New York Herald* when he met Livingstone, then searching for the sources of the Nile, at Ujiji, on Lake Tanganyika, in 1871

Letter 57

From Nettie to Celie. Nettie praises Samuel's wisdom and kindness. She is enthusiastic about the ship on which they crossed the Atlantic, and about the strange ways of England, where some fund-raising was done. She is beginning to learn about the colonial history of Africa. She has discovered that slaves transported to America were often bought from within the slave-trade practised by Africans. The journey from England is via Lisbon, Dakar and Monrovia.

NOTES AND GLOSSARY:

J. A. Rogers:	Joel Augustus Rogers (1883–1966), historian and journalist. His *From Superman to Man* was published in 1917. His controversial views on African history met with opposition
vesper service:	evening church service

Letter 58

From Nettie to Celie. She recounts more about the journey, including the stop in Senegal, then a French colony, and the visit to Monrovia. Nettie finds that there are many white men in Africa, and that not all are missionaries. The president of the African-governed state of Liberia seems remote from the problems of his people. Nettie hears the singing of exhausted workers in the cacao fields and learns that the plantations are Dutch-owned. She ends by describing the intense emotion of homecoming when she, Corrine and Samuel first saw the coast of Africa and kneeled to give thanks to God.

NOTES AND GLOSSARY:
Senegalese: Wolof and Fulani are spoken in Senegal
Tubman: this must be a predecessor of the noted President (William V. S.) Tubman (1895–1971), who took office in 1944
cacoa: the cacao tree; its seeds are used to make cocoa and chocolate

Letter 59

Celie resumes her letters to God. When Shug pleads with her not to murder Albert, on the grounds that his removal would leave her only Grady to sleep with, Celie begs Shug to sleep with her in future, and Shug agrees.

NOTES AND GLOSSARY:
Thou Shalt Not Kill: not Christ's words, but the sixth of the Ten Commandments; Deuteronomy 5:17

Letter 60

Celie and Shug sleep together 'like sisters' because Celie is too angry, at the thought of the letterless years, to make love. Shug persuades her to sew herself some pants; her dress is unsuitable for work in the fields, and pants will suit her.

NOTES AND GLOSSARY:
Don't git uppity: don't become insolent

Letter 61

Celie is looking forward to Nettie's return, but is beginning to worry about her children, fearing that their conception (which she believes to have been incestuous), may have injured their development. She quotes within this letter to God an entire letter from Nettie.

Nettie describes how they left the ship at a small port somewhere in West Africa and were led to the village where they are to work. The land of Olinka is described. The people are amazed by the sight of the women missionaries, and they gather round Nettie and Corrine, touching their dresses and hair. Their guide, Joseph, explains that the missionaries who have come before were all white, and furthermore, only men have come this far. The Olinka ask questions of the women, and one comments that the two children resemble Nettie, not Corrine. The Olinka are healthy but very poor by American standards. They harvest enough yams, cassava and other produce to keep them self-sufficient. They count themselves rich in roofleaf, the covering for their huts, and their 'god', since they worship the leaf as a symbol of divine protection.

NOTES AND GLOSSARY:

dunces:	she fears they may be mentally handicapped
pidgin English:	a trade-language drawing grammar and vocabulary from English and other sources; it often serves as a medium between speakers of different West African languages
bush:	forest or uncultivated countryside
palm wine:	made from fermented palm sap
cassava ... yam:	plants with starchy tubers
millet:	a type of food grain

Letter 62

From Nettie to Celie. Nettie seldom has time to put pen to paper, but whatever she is doing, she is writing to Celie in her mind. She writes realistically about West African insect bites and other difficulties of settling in, including cultural differences. Olivia is the only girl in the village school because the Olinka believe that education should be for boys alone. Olivia compares this narrow-mindedness with that of 'white people at home who don't want colored people to learn'. She hopes that she and her Olinka friend Tashi will grow up to have more interesting lives than women are allowed in the village. Corrine is becoming jealous of Nettie as a rival. Domestic troubles seem to be in store.

NOTES AND GLOSSARY:

Schweitzer:	Dr Albert Schweitzer (1875–1965), German theologian, philosopher and musician, who abandoned a brilliant career in 1913, to run a mission-hospital at Lambaréné (in present-day Gabon)

Letter 63

From Nettie to Celie. Tashi's parents complain that Olivia's influence is distancing their daughter from the life and customs of the Olinka people. Nettie tells Tashi's father that Africa is changing and will soon be more than just a man's world. He defends the dignity of Olinka women; superior, he says, to the condition of an outcast and drudge such as Nettie. He says he is willing to receive Olivia in his house, where she will be able to learn true womanly ways.

NOTES AND GLOSSARY:

we send him women: women to be used as prostitutes

Letter 64

From Nettie to Celie. Five years more have passed. A road is being built through the forest. The Olinka welcome the road-builders with gifts and friendship. Corrine is growing more jealous of Nettie, and has asked her not to invite Samuel to her hut. Nettie now values the company of her niece and nephew more than ever. Tashi has lost her father, who died of malaria. Nettie broods about the lives of Olinka women, who seem happy although they have to share husbands and cannot have men as friends. She thinks the women spoil their husbands and that this makes the men 'childish'. She also notes that Olinka men have the power of life and death over their women.

NOTES AND GLOSSARY:

Uncle Remus:	Joel Chandler Harris (1848–1908) published *Uncle Remus, his Songs and Sayings* in 1881, and the classic series of Uncle Remus books followed. An old black American tells stories to a small boy. Among the animal characters drawn from black folk-tales are Brer (Brother) Rabbit and Brer Fox. Like Alice Walker, he was born in Eatonton, Georgia
keening:	lamentation for the dead

Letter 65

From Nettie to Celie. Another year has passed. The road the Olinka welcomed has flattened most of their village. The whole region, furthermore, has been bought by a British company and the forests are being cleared for rubber plantations. The chief's appeal to the governor only resulted in a demand for taxes. Essential village buildings, including the school, have been rebuilt, however; several girls now attend the school. Corrine has been ill.

Letter 66

From Nettie to Celie. Times are becoming ever more difficult. Corrine frets because the children resemble Nettie. She demands that Nettie and Samuel swear on the Bible that they never had an affair. The fields and hunting grounds of the Olinka have been destroyed to make space for planting rubber.

Letter 67

From Nettie to Celie. Samuel has always thought that the children must be Nettie's. That is why he first took her in and later invited her to go to Africa. Samuel turns out to possess crucial information about the sisters' background. When he was a young man, he used to be acquainted with Alphonso. He is sure that Nettie and Celie are the children not of Alphonso but of a trader lynched by white rivals. Alphonso married this man's widow, who was afflicted by mental illness. This woman must be Celie and Nettie's mother and Alphonso their stepfather. Nettie prays that this letter may reach Celie with the wonderful news that 'Pa is not our pa!'

Letter 68

This brief note is Celie's last letter to God until Letter 90. It records her amazed and delighted discovery that her children were not incestuously conceived, and that all her assumptions about family have been turned upside down. Shug is going to take her away, to Tennessee. She ends by telling God that he must be asleep, to have kept all this from her.

Letter 69

From Celie to Nettie. Celie visits Alphonso. She and Shug drive there in the Packard, wearing their new 'flower pants' as emblems of liberation. There are real flowers everywhere about them as they drive through the countryside on the new tarmac roads. Alphonso seems to be enjoying great prosperity; he has a new, fifteen-year-old wife. He has a white man working in his store. He says that he kept the true story of Celie's parentage secret because it was too sad to tell to little girls. Shug and Celie look for but cannot find the graves of Celie's parents.

NOTES AND GLOSSARY:
bought me my own white boy: hired a white man as an assistant; Alphonso characteristically employs the language of slavery
cockleburrs: prickly plants

Letter 70

From Nettie to Celie. Corrine is dying. Nettie has told her about the children's parentage, but she cannot believe it, or remember the meeting with Celie in the store (in Letter 10).

Letter 71

From Nettie to Celie. Nettie has tried to make Corrine remember. She has found in Corrine's trunk the quilt she made from the cloth she bought the day she met Celie; this revives a memory long suppressed, as Corrinne now admits, because Celie was so like Olivia. She recalls the incident with the white storekeeper that Celie writes of in Letter 10. Corrine dies just after acknowledging that Nettie has told the truth.

NOTES AND GLOSSARY:
hitching post: to tie horses
appliquéd: in needlework, pieces of one material applied to the surface of another
Spelman Seminary: see Part 1, The author's life, p. 5, above

Letter 72

From Nettie to Celie. Corrine is given a traditional Olinka funeral. Samuel and the children feel their loss keenly. Nettie dreams of seeing Celie again. Two ill-mannered white men have been to survey the village. Nettie has told Samuel about her letter-writing.

NOTES AND GLOSSARY:
my friend: menstrual period
one ritual: circumcision
faces painted white: the colour of death and mourning in many parts of Africa

Letter 73

From Celie to Nettie. Celie has stopped writing to God because, she says, 'if he ever listened to poor colored women the world would be a different place'. In spite of her reputation as 'a devil', Shug dissuades Celie from blasphemy. They discuss religion. Celie admits that her idea of God was a mental picture of an old grey-bearded white man. Shug tells her that God is not a person outside her but a power within. God can be seen in the beauty of nature. He can even be known through sexual pleasure, 'some of the best stuff God did'. Shug believes that God wants to be admired. If people pass a field of purple without noticing, she says, 'it pisses God off'. Above all the idea of God as male has to be abandoned. That falsifies one's views of everything.

Letter 74

From Celie to Nettie. Celie relates the story of Sofia, who is out of prison and restored to her family, although now almost a stranger to her children. Shug and Celie announce that they are going to Memphis, Tennessee. Celie denounces Albert for robbing her of Nettie: she is leaving him to 'enter the Creation'. Mary Agnes is leaving Harpo to go north as a singer. Sofia is called back to look after the mayor's family, but undertakes on her return to look after Harpo and his child by Mary Agnes, named Jolentha but known as Suzie Q. The women have taken charge.

NOTES AND GLOSSARY:
sassing:	being insolent to
dime:	a coin worth ten cents
bangs:	fringes of hair
Prob-limbszzzz:	problems

Letter 75

From Celie to Nettie. Shug, Celie, Mary Agnes and Grady are travelling to Memphis. Grady is now infatuated with Mary Agnes. Albert reacts badly to Celie's departure, heaping insults on her. In return she curses him: she threatens that everything will turn out badly for him until he recognises his crimes and decides to treat her properly.

Letter 76

From Celie to Nettie. Shug owns a big house in Memphis, decorated throughout with figures and designs of elephants and turtles. The friends cook and listen to music. The newspapers show them how badly the world is being managed. Celie becomes obsessed with making pants. A few can be made for tolerable men, such as Odessa's husband Jack. Shug encourages her to start a business, selling brightly coloured pants to women everywhere.

NOTES AND GLOSSARY:
collards:	leaves of a cabbage-like vegetable
souse:	pigs' trotters and other parts, pickled
okra:	a vegetable also known as 'ladies' fingers'
betsy bugs:	small insects

Letter 77

From Celie to Nettie. Celie now has all she desires except the safe return of Nettie and the children. Her firm, 'Folkspants, Unlimited', is prospering. She has two assistants, twins called Jerene and Darlene. Darlene is trying to teach her correct English. She tries to make Celie say 'we' rather than 'us' when Celie says 'us not so hot'. Celie is planning a pair of pants for Sofia, one leg red and the other purple.

Letter 78

From Celie to Nettie. Sofia's mother has died. Although pall-bearers at funerals have always been men, Sofia fights a successful battle against male prejudice, and she and her sisters carry the coffin to the grave. Celie is now much altered by Shug's influence: she teaches Harpo and Sofia how to smoke 'reefer'. Celie says that she takes the drug when she wants to talk to God or to make love. Sofia is shocked. They sit round the kitchen table and smoke reefers until they hear a mysterious humming, which may, perhaps, be the murmur of the universe.

NOTES AND GLOSSARY:

pass: die
fight the good fight: from the hymn, 'Fight the good fight/With all thy might', by Fr. J. S. B. Monsell (1811–75)
glory: heaven
reefer: a marijuana cigarette

Letter 79

From Celie to Nettie. Albert has reformed. He is now clean and hardworking, and even does housework and cooking. It seems that he deteriorated rapidly after Celie left him. He was rescued, however, by Harpo, who showed him great kindness. Harpo also made him return all Celie's remaining letters from Nettie, so lifting the effect of her curse.

NOTES AND GLOSSARY:

yall must still be dope: you must still be doped
a hard row to hoe: difficult to deal with
cut my own switch: prepare my own punishment

Letter 80

From Nettie to Celie. Nettie is plump and gray-haired, and is now married to Samuel. The Olinka have been forced from their village by the rubber planters, and have to settle on a barren strip of land with no water supply for six months of the year. They suffer further indignity when they are reduced to buying tin to replace the sacred roofleaf. It is no surprise that they have lost whatever faith they may have had in missionaries. Nettie, Samuel and the children travel to England to seek help for the Olinka. On the journey, they meet the English lady who had been working as a missionary when they first arrived years before. She is returning to England to retire as she is now sixty-five, and she speaks of her early life in English upper-class society and how she sought escape from married life in England in missionary work. On arrival in England, Samuel and Nettie attend a meeting with a bishop whose only concern is the relationship between them now that Corrine is dead. He does not even consider the plight of the Olinka. Afterwards, Samuel talks of his doubts about their work, and reminisces about his early life with Corrine. He breaks down in tears, and in comforting him, Nettie reveals her love for him. They are married soon afterwards. Olivia reveals that Adam is unhappy in England because he misses Tashi. He is worried about her, as, in a gesture of support for traditional Olinka customs, she intends to undergo ritual facial scarring and circumcision. It seems clear that Adam loves Tashi.

NOTES AND GLOSSARY:

Fall:	autumn
a big war:	the year seems to be 1938 or 1939. See Part 4, pp. 69–70, for a discussion of the chronology of the novel
milkfed:	feeble, effeminate
bloody cutting:	circumcision
the Belgian Congo:	the colonial name for what is now the Republic of Zaire. See the note on King Leopold, below
antimacassared:	protected by an embroidered covering
Edward duBoyce:	W(illiam) E(dward) B(urghardt) Du Bois (pronounced Du Boyce) (c. 1868–1963), scholar, poet and Pan-Africanist. He was the first black American to obtain a Harvard doctorate
King Leopold:	Leopold II (1835–1909), King of the Belgians (1865–1909); recognised in 1885 as sovereign of the Congo Free State, annexed as the Belgian Congo in 1908

Letter 81

From Nettie to Celie. Nettie and Samuel have returned from England to Olinka. Tashi has undergone the traditional initiation ceremonies, but has become ashamed of the marks on her face. Adam refuses to speak to her. He is desperate to return to America.

Letter 82

From Celie to Nettie. Alphonso's wife calls Celie to tell her that he is dead. The house and the business he ran were in fact owned by Celie's father, so they now belong to Celie and Nettie. Celie and Shug go to look at the house, and when they get there Celie finds Alphonso's tombstone which declares him to have been kind to the poor and helpless. Celie cannot believe that the beautiful house they find now belongs to her.

Letter 83

From Celie to Nettie. Celie is broken-hearted because Shug has fallen in love with a young man called Germaine. Celie had spent the summer in Memphis working on the house she inherited in preparation for Nettie's arrival. When she returns, Shug talks eagerly about this nineteen-year-old, who plays the flute in her band, until Celie's evident grief checks her enthusiasm. She pleads for six months' grace: the affair cannot last longer than that. Celie grieves jealously nonetheless. Grady and Mary Agnes are growing marijuana in Panama.

NOTES AND GLOSSARY:

fortune cookies:	they have 'fortunes' written on thin slips of paper inserted before baking
flittish name:	fancy name
buns:	buttocks
boocoos:	(*French*) *beaucoup*, a lot

Letter 84

From Celie to Nettie. Sofia's youngest child (not Harpo's), Henrietta, is very ill. Caring for her helps to keep Celie from despair at Shug's infidelity. A diet of yams is prescribed, following African custom advocated by Nettie in a letter, but the child cannot stand the taste, so it has to be cunningly disguised. Celie and Albert draw closer together; talking about Shug is a bond between them. Albert proposes that they resume married life, but Celie speaks frankly, at last, of her physical repugnance at the sight of naked men.

Letter 85

From Celie to Nettie. An official telegram reports that Nettie and family are believed drowned after the ship bringing them from Africa was sunk by German mines. All Celie's letters to Nettie have, at the same time, been returned unopened.

Letter 86

From Nettie to Celie. Tashi and her mother have run away to join a group of rebels against white rule, known as *mbeles*. The Olinka are falling sick because the destruction of their yam crops has removed their resistance to malaria. Nettie is full of worries and hopes about returning to America. She fears that Celie may be living in wretched conditions. She expects that life will be hard for her own family once back in the United States. But there will be much to discuss, says Nettie, always a teacher, including her evolving conception of God. Africa has taught her to think of God as a Spirit unconstrained by the images of one religion or another, to be seen in Christ or in roofleaf. The letter ends with the dramatic news that Adam has gone away in search of Tashi.

NOTES AND GLOSSARY:
Nearly thirty years: a useful clue to the novel's time-scheme. The present date appears to be 1940 or 1941
To Be or Not to Be: *Hamlet*, Act III, Scene 1

Letter 87

Celie to Nettie. Celie stands naked before her mirror, contemplating the changes brought by the years, because she is afraid that Shug no longer loves her. Shug and Germaine are touring the country. Albert, although still known to Celie only as Mr. ——, is now her only friend at hand. She finds that in spite of all the wrongs he has done her she cannot hate him. He has reformed, and he too loves Shug. He protects Celie from the unwanted attentions of men Sofia and Harpo put in her way. Celie and Albert sit and reminisce, about earlier events in their lives together.

Sofia still has troubles. Miss Eleanor Jane, the mayor's daughter brought up by Sofia, is still devoted to her. Eleanor Jane keeps visiting Sofia, bringing her husband and baby and demanding admiration. Sofia would prefer to be left alone. After her sufferings she cannot accept this white woman as a friend, and she is too honest to pretend to feel warmth towards the baby. Other black women pretend, she tells Eleanor Jane, because they are afraid of whites.

Shug writes, describing her travels. Celie is angry with her, but tries to accept Shug's right to her own life. She and Albert talk about Shug. Albert says she is 'manly', but Celie thinks that her virtues are womanly. They also talk about pants, symbolic, they agree, of freedom and power in modern America. Celie tells him how men wear robes in Africa. Civilisation there is profoundly different in other ways. Africans believe that the first man was black and created long before Adam. The Olinka, she has heard from Nettie, worship the snake. Albert finds her good company.

NOTES AND GLOSSARY:

the trees with you: God on your side (since Shug has taught her that God is present in Nature)

cotton gin: a machine to separate seeds and other impurities from cotton; a symbol of white oppression of black people

cracker: biscuit

zamine: examines

adobe: Shug describes a house made of sun-dried brick of clay and straw

a scanless: scandalously

Omatangu: the first man, in African myth

Letter 88

From Nettie to Celie. Adam has brought Tashi home, protesting, from the rebels' camp. He caught up with and accompanied her and her mother to the *mbeles* encampment. He persuaded them to return with him. Tashi is afraid to marry Adam because she thinks Americans will despise her. But Adam has his face marked with carvings like hers: he has become Adam Omatangu, Adam of Africa. Samuel then marries Adam and Tashi, and the whole family set out for the coast to find a ship bound for home.

Letter 89

From Celie to Nettie. Shug has been trying to get news of Nettie from the State Department, but the men there are racialists and uncooperative. Celie has not lost hope that Nettie may be alive. Sofia is working in the store Celie and Nettie have inherited. She scares the white man hired in Alphonso's time. Eleanor Jane is caring for Henrietta. She has at long last found out the circumstances in which Sofia went to work for her family. Sofia thinks there is hope for Eleanor Jane yet. Albert sits on his verandah, sewing. He is designing a shirt to match Celie's pants. Shug's return home makes Celie happy, for the moment. Shug explains that Germaine has been sent away to college. Celie tells her that she has been spending time with Albert, who she mentions by name for the first time.

Letter 90

'Dear God . . . Dear Everything', Celie writes. Nettie and the children are home, to the happiest of reunions. Even Albert is included, as he counts now as 'family'. Mary Agnes has left Grady, and returned from Panama to look after Suzie Q. Tashi and Adam are admired by all. Celie knows that the young people think that she and her friends are old, but she thinks 'this the youngest us ever felt'.

Part 3

Commentary

Nature, purpose and achievement

Some readers will value *The Color Purple* as a committed, feminist work; others may enjoy it as a good story, without accepting all its assumptions. It is, indeed, an unusual example of a novel with two different kinds of appeal. In some respects it is a challenging and shocking book, radical and very up-to-date in attitudes and ideas. In other ways it is a traditional and even old-fashioned story. This mixture of qualities may help to explain its remarkable success with a wide readership.

The novel has aroused keen controversy, especially in the United States. Some hostile critics object to the portrayal of the love affair between Celie and Shug, either because they object to the sympathetic treatment of homosexuality, or because they think it evades the hard questions that arise from Celie's story. Others object to the remorseless depiction of acts of male violence against women in a novel about black people. Some American critics have argued that Alice Walker threatens to divide the black community and detract from the struggle against racialism. Walker's onslaught against all forms of male aggression (religion included) has attracted much sympathy, not only from women readers, and won champions who defend and acclaim every aspect of the book.

Admirers and detractors are often so concerned with social issues that they treat the novel as a battleground for debate rather than a work of literature with strengths and weaknesses of composition. The author is so strongly committed to the righting of a particular wrong, that readers are bound to react to the obvious and pervasive bias of a fictional world where men are (almost always) silly and vicious, while women are thoughtful, generous and brave. If we are to read and criticise effectively, however, we must accept the author's bias and see what sort of fiction she has made of it, remembering that a novel has to be written from some point of view. No novelist surveys the whole of life dispassionately.

At the heart of the story a man is denouncing his wife: 'You black, you pore, you ugly, you a woman. Goddam, he say, you nothing at all' (Letter 75). The whole novel can be seen as an attack on the assumptions behind these words of Albert to Celie, just before she leaves him to start a new life with Shug. The novel shows that poverty and even ugliness can be overcome; once emancipated, Celie grows rich and thinks better of her appearance. The central theme, that blackness and womanhood are rich and beautiful endowments, is asserted throughout, often in lively and dramatic scenes, skilfully planned and written. One of Alice Walker's aims is to expose racial injustice, which is plain to see in many of the American and African episodes. But her first purpose is to assert that all women are sisters, and to show how the bond between women can help them to overcome their oppressors and emancipate themselves, winning through to an independence that is social and economic, and spiritual as well. The novelist's powers of composition are considered under the headings of Structure, Style and Characters in later sections of this Commentary. One positive feature of her achievement is crucial to the success of the whole and requires to be mentioned here.

The fictional presentation of violence is very difficult. Inferior writing is often unrealistic when trying to arouse pity, because over-insistence and repetition (blows raining on blows) tend to weaken the effect, while more realistic writing often appeals to emotions other than pity. Walker's purposes in this novel require her to portray many incidents of rape and beating, but these are so carefully and tactfully described that the effect is realistic and pitiful. She pictures grotesque aspects of violence in Celie's accounts of how she has been abused (in Letter 47, for example), and the inanity of violence in the descriptions of Sofia's fights with Harpo (Letter 20, for example). Letter 37 depicts an extremely emotive scene: a black woman strikes a white official, and the police close in on her. The power of such an incident to arouse emotion docs not make it easier to render successfully, without stereotyped effects. Celie's halting description, interrupted by Albert when she breaks down, is simple and strong. More space is given, on the next page, to Celie's caring for Sofia in prison than to her beating and arrest. *The Color Purple* depicts many scenes of violence, but it is a tender rather than a violent book.

Serious commitment to a cause and popular story-telling have always been compatible, but the mixture can involve dangers. We accept the author's right to shape the story towards its happy ending. Corrine dies (repentant, after all her false suspicions) just in time for Nettie to marry Samuel. We do not imagine that anything improper ever occurred between them, because we understand that nothing must detract from the virtue of the 'good' characters. (Shug's escapade with a young man introduces a refreshing touch of cold reality towards the end.) We may be less willing to accept scenes where the author seems to have managed the evidence for her argument in the course of shaping the story: Tashi's father is a banal spokesman for keeping Africa a man's world; soon after opposing Nettie he scorns Western medicine and dies of malaria. Readers familiar with Chinua Achebe's novels know that a tribal elder might have been subtler in argument and physically more resilient, if Alice Walker had allowed. When the bishop who receives Samuel and Nettie in England proves to be foolish and feeble, we are unsurprised because he is obviously akin to

Tashi's father in the novel's scheme, which always leaves Nettie in the right. We are equally unsurprised when Celie's business rapidly succeeds, because that is also required for the happy ending. The danger is that we may feel the author is indulging 'her' characters in ways that undermine her case: we may reflect that missionary work and small businesses, women's roles in African society, and new bearings in theology, are all more difficult and more interesting than Nettie and Celie are permitted to find out. Such thoughts are liable to arise in reading the last series of letters; if that happens, the demands of the happy ending have weakened the novel's themes.

In other ways, however, the novel derives strength from its reworking of old and reliable conventions for new purposes. Literature constantly renews itself in this way, and Alice Walker has a sure sense of how to tell a story. Not all committed writers are so good-humoured. Her sense of fun adds to many scenes: 'Folkspants, Unlimited' might have become an over-worked symbolic ploy in a less deft and exuberant writer. She is unafraid of sentimentality, knowing the part it must play in the kind of tale she has to tell. Steven Spielberg's film version reminds us, by contrast, how restrained and effective is sentiment in the happy ending of the book. (See pp. 63–4, in Part 4 below, for comments on the film.)

The novel is dedicated to 'the Spirit', and God is vaguely present in the background. Readers reactions here will vary according to the attitudes they bring to their reading, but these are not likely to be greatly changed. (See pp. 68–9, in Part 4 below, for further comments on the novel's treatment of religion.) In this respect, as in others, the novel is too recent and enmeshed in controversy for any general agreement to be reached at present about its place in American literature.

Background to composition

Alice Walker wrote an essay called 'Writing *The Color Purple*' in 1982 (reissued in *In Search of Our Mothers' Gardens*, p. 355). She describes there how her characters seemed to live in her imagination while she was working on the novel, seeming to her like real people, 'trying to contact me, to speak through me'. The characters refused to collaborate with the author in New York or San Francisco, where she made two false starts: 'that was when I knew for sure that these were country people'. A rural retreat in Northern California suited them better because it was like Georgia; among the goats and the hay, 'Celie began, haltingly, to speak'.

The country setting might have been taken for granted. Alice Walker had already turned the Georgia of her childhood into her fictional world. Her first novel, *The Third Life of Grange Copeland*, covers three generations of a Georgian family between the 1920s and the 1960s. Its villain, Brownfield, anticipates the brutal male characters of *The Color*

Purple: he shoots his wife in the face because he cannot bear the thought that she has a life of her own. The heroine of *Meridian* works in the Civil Rights Movement for the rights of poor black people in the Deep South. Many of Walker's short stories depict the same rural Southern settings as the novels. Roselily in the opening story of *In Love and Trouble* is a poor black girl living in a remote region of the South: unmarried with three children, she is prepared to marry a most unsuitable husband for the sake of respectability; this girl is in some ways a prototype of the young Celie. Alice Walker has often spoken of her debt to stories told by her mother and grandparents. One of her motives for writing is to help to keep such stories alive; they in turn have animated her fiction from the first. Celie and the other members of *The Color Purple*'s cast came to her from her memories as well as from her imagination.

'Writing *The Color Purple*' also comments on how the book was conceived as a historical novel:

> In an interview discussing my work a black male critic said he'd heard I might write a historical novel some day, and went on to say, in effect: Heaven Protect Us From It.

She was amused because her idea of a historical novel was unconventional: she began not with a grand historical design, but with a chance remark by her sister about a woman's underwear. Walker holds serious views, nonetheless, about the place of women during the later nineteenth and earlier twentieth century: these were women of the hopeless generations, as she wrote in the title-essay of *In Search of Our Mothers' Gardens*, 'suspended in a time in history where the options for Black women were severely limited'.

> And they either kill themselves or they are used up by the man, or by the children or by ... whatever the pressures against them. And they cannot go anywhere ... And that's the way I see many of the women I have created in fiction. They are closer to my mother's generation than to mine. They had few choices.

(See pp. 6–8, General background, in Part 1 above, for more details of this thesis.) The men of this 'suspended' time hindered rather than helped because they tended to retain mental attitudes belonging to the era of slavery, especially if they happened to be sons or grandsons of overseers or slave owners. *Living by the Word* includes a reply to a woman who asked about the character of Albert; Walker wrote there, 'it is clear that Mr. ——'s father is part white; this is how Mister comes by his run-down plantation house' (p. 81). We are often reminded in *The Color Purple* of how black and white Southerners are sometimes more closely related than the whites want to admit; Mary Agnes's visit to the prison warden (in Letters 40–1) shows such a relationship. Walker's belief that white slavers'

contempt for their 'servants' lingered on in the contemptuous attitudes of
some black (as well as white) men towards women, and may not yet be
extinct, is one reason for hostility among male critics to her treatment of
history in *The Color Purple*.

Alice Walker had long been an active member of the Civil Rights
Movement when she came to write her third novel, and she no longer
cared about what male hostility her work might arouse. She meant to write
on behalf of her people, but on the women's side of every question. She
wrote in *Meridian* about 'the song of the people, transformed by the
experience of each generation that holds them together, and if any part of
it is lost the people suffer and are without soul' (pp. 205–6). She also
declared:

> I am preoccupied with the spiritual survival, the survival *whole* of
> my people, but beyond that, I am committed to exploring the oppres-
> sions, the insanities, the loyalties, and the triumphs of black women. *(In
> Search of Our Mothers' Gardens, p. 250)*

This remained the author's ideological position when she settled down in
Northern California to listen to her characters. There must have been
another thought in her mind. Her previous books had been well received,
but had not made her famous or financially secure. She wanted to write a
best-seller, and knew that in this next novel she could succeed.

Structure and themes

The structure of *The Color Purple* is underlined by the repetition and
linking of its important themes. The story is firmly constructed, with a
desperately dramatic opening, a middle full of conflict and endeavour, and
a happy ending. It is an old-fashioned kind of story. It begins with the
breakup of a family and ends with its reunion: loving sisters are parted, but
restored to each other in spite of all the treacherous efforts of the villain.
Mother and children, torn apart by cruelty, are also reunited, in hap-
pier circumstances than could ever have been expected. Virtue is further
rewarded, in the cases of Celie and Nettie, by the unlooked-for and timely
inheritance of house and property (hitherto wrongly withheld from them).

Much of the action depends on coincidence: not only is Nettie
befriended by the adoptive parents of Celie's children; Samuel happens
(rather improbably given their respective characters and ways of life) to
have been an old crony of Alphonso. Furthermore, this means that he
knows the secret of the sisters' parentage. The stain of incest is thus
removed; Alphonso turns out to be an evil stepfather, as we might have
expected. Albert is dramatically changed into a reformed character at the
end – an amiable avuncular appendage to the large, prosperous, matriar-
chal family circle – completing the reconciliations, and preventing any

animosity from lingering. The story is likely to remind us, especially in its rather lengthy closing stages, of the ways in which Victorian melodrama pitted brute force against love and friendship, leaving heroes and heroines well off in every way.

The title points to the imaginative design. Purple is the colour of a bruise. When Sofia has been beaten by the police she is the colour of 'an eggplant' (Letter 38). Purple is also the colour of the robes of royalty and nobility, of Roman emperors and English lords. This is why Celie thinks it the colour Shug Avery would choose to wear: 'She like a queen to me, so I say to [Albert's sister] Kate, Somethin purple, maybe little red in it too' (Letter 12). Red goes with purple, in stately robes and imperial pomp. There is no purple in the store, and even red would be too expensive for Albert; but Celie later makes pants of purple, red, and every other bright colour. Purple has a third significance in the novel, as an example of God's power; a symbol of Shug's religion in Letter 73. But it is the contrast between the bruised and battered victims that women often are and the queenly, triumphant figures they can become when they are free that gives *The Color Purple* its basic structure.

This is reflected in the structure of Celie's story. She first appears raped and beaten, humbly appealing to God for a sign. The last letter begins with an almost priestly address to God and the 'Creation' to which Celie now feels united: 'Dear God ... dear peoples. Dear Everything'. A sense of benediction pervades Letter 90; few novels have more warmly coloured happy endings. The story traces Celie's gradual emancipation from Albert's despotic rule. Encouraged by Nettie and Sofia to 'fight', she needs the sense of confidence and security provided by Shug's love, together with her fury at Albert's theft of the letters from Nettie, before she is able to fight her way free from drudgery, and 'enter into the Creation' (Letter 74).

Celie's story is linked with those of the other women who achieve emancipation, but chiefly with the misfortunes of Sofia. Sofia's story shows how skilfully the planning of a sequence of incidents can be managed. She makes her first appearance, in Letter 17, 'marching ... like going to war', hand in hand with Harpo, but a little in front. It is this independent approach to life that goads Celie into her one act of betrayal:

Beat her. I say.
Next time us see Harpo his face a mess of bruises. (Letter 19)

Harpo is the one to wear the colour purple in the form of bruises, for the time being. Celie's penitence and her reconciliation with Sofia follow, in Letter 21; but if we think that fighting is funny when it is the man who gets the worst of it, there are warnings that we ought to think again. Letter 20 shows Sofia and Harpo grotesquely locked in a futile struggle. Letter 36 gives us the picture of Mary Agnes when Sofia has hit her, a tooth hanging from her mouth, blood and slobber on her face. Sofia's fisticuffs are not to be seen as heroic, but as the unhealthy product of the violence of her upbringing. When she is beaten by the police, as described in the next letter, we recall Celie's two words of betrayal. Neither Celie nor Mary Agnes is implicated in what happens to Sofia, but their acts of aggression, Celie's 'Beat her' and Squeak's slap, are connected with Sofia's exchange of blows with the mayor, since all result from the violent world of narrow-minded male supremacy in which the characters have lived.

Sofia's imprisonment, the subject of the next series of letters, is an ordeal involving all three women, so that their achievement of dignity and independence at the end of the novel is a shared achievement, and their three stories appear as components in a unified whole. Celie makes purple and red pants for Sofia and dreams of her wearing them and 'jumping over the moon' (Letter 77). Celie has her room painted purple and red (Letter 89). Celie and Sofia richly deserve to celebrate their freedom after what they have endured. The colour of bruises has beome the noblest of colours by the end of the American section of the novel.

The African section is linked with the American in many ways, so that this wide-ranging novel remains unified. One connection is the theme of female emancipation. Nettie escapes from fear and oppression, first to Samuel's protection, then to a new life of worthwhile service in Africa (looking after Celie's children as well as those in her school), and finally to a happy marriage. She says (in Letter 62) that whatever she is doing, she is always writing to Celie. She needed Celie's self-sacrifice and practical help in her early years; during the long separation she is still supported by the knowledge of her sister's love. The juxtaposition of letters to God and letters between sisters, when Celie begins to write to Nettie (in Letter 69), is no accident: they find spiritual comfort and endurance through writing to each other. Other interconnections arise from ways in which the family is physically parted yet still in some ways connected. Nettie sees Celie in Olivia's face. The void made by the loss of Celie's children begins to be filled when Nettie can tell her about them; Albert's attempt to deny Celie a part of her life is foiled when Nettie, Olivia and Adam return at the close.

The African and American settings are further linked by the novel's historical themes. Nettie expresses the strong emotion of black Americans towards the continent from which their ancestors were brought as slaves. The one attitude of the Olinka people that Nettie cannot endure is their refusal to discuss what took place in Africa during the era of the slave trade. However unpleasant the subject, she believes, it must be treated honestly: she acknowledges that Africans as well as Europeans bought and sold slaves. Tashi weeps when she hears that Olivia's grandmother was a slave in America, but other Africans ignore the issue, accepting no respon-sibility. That is, perhaps, understandable, given that the Olinka are victims of history in a different but almost as horrifying manner. Their fields are destroyed by the coming of the road and the rubber plantations. We are reminded of how ruthlessly modernisation has often been imposed in Africa, and we are shown that here, as in America, black people and white are to blame for injustice: the black members of the Liberian government and the white administrators of European commercial projects are equally unconcerned about 'the natives'. Yet in Africa as in America 'the world is changing' and in some respects for the better, in offering new opportunities to women. Nettie tells Tashi's father, 'It is no longer a world just for boys and men' (Letter 63). The Olinka men do not welcome the idea of equal opportunities for girls and boys: in this they are condemned, by Olivia, in the strongest terms, when she says they are as narrow-minded as the white racialists in America (Letter 62). The end of the story shows hope for Africa and America, however, when Adam and Tashi arrive in Georgia with the traditional tribal marks proudly worn on their faces to express the independence and determination of a new, united generation.

Shug gives a new significance to the colour purple when she explains her religious belief in Letter 73, saying that God is offended if people walk past a field of purple flowers without noticing. Thoughts of God, orthodox and unconventional, are present throughout the story, most of which is addressed to him (or 'it' as Shug would say), and this strengthens the novel's unity. Nettie lives a dedicated life as a missionary, and Celie's emancipation is presented in religious terms. Celie abandons the concept of God as an old white man; Nettie's experience agrees with this: 'God is different to us now . . . More spirit than ever before' (Letter 86).

The use of letters also contributes to the structure. It provides two points of view, and two styles, in the first-person narrators, Celie and Nettie. Because letter writing (and the theft of letters) is part of the story, the sisters sustaining each other by writing, and so sharing in an act of faith, the epistolary medium adds to the novel's unity. Use of letters also affects the distribution of incidents in time. The events of a few days are described in one or more of Celie's letters, and then years pass unrecorded. Some of these intervals are noted in the letters; others are not. We sometimes have to calculate the passage of time for ourselves, not without difficulty. (The interval between Letters 44 and 45, for example, is hard to determine.) This elliptical method is effective in dealing with the challenge Alice Walker set herself of presenting nearly forty years, from two lives spent mostly apart, in the space of a relatively short novel (about seventy thousand words). There are imperfections in the handling of some of the material involved. Nettie's encounter with Sofia (described in Letter 55) occurs within a year of her running away, but many years later in Sofia's story. (Those interested will find more about timing on pp. 69–70, in Part 4 below.) Flaws of this kind do not, however, interfere with the fundamental structure of the novel.

Style

The Color Purple belongs to a long tradition of American fiction, going back to *Huckleberry Finn* (1884) by Mark Twain (pseudonym of Samuel Langhorne Clemens, 1835–1910). In novels of this kind a young or innocent narrator tells the story in dialect and uneducated English and with a much less mature understanding than the one that the reader can share with the author. *The Catcher in the Rye* (1951) by J. D. Salinger (*b.* 1919) is another such work. The style of these young narrators has the attractions of lively speech. Like Twain's Huck Finn and Salinger's Holden Caulfield, the young Celie writes the early letters in a style close to the way she speaks, and although her later writing matures, it does not lose its frank appeal. The earliest letters establish her in our sympathy. They often have a breathless immediacy:

> Dear God
> He act like he can't stand me no more. Say I'm evil an always up to no good. He took my other little baby, a boy this time. But I don't think he kilt it. (Letter 3)

Declining to name 'him' seems natural: this is how children talk. This style adds to the concentrated impact of the opening letters, and anyway, God knows who she is talking about.

Some of the best writing in the novel comes in Celie's curt notes on the horrific world she grows up in:

> His wife died. She was kilt by her boyfriend coming home from church. (Letter 4)

This is how she introduces the murder of Harpo's mother, an episode more fully described in later letters. The childish brevity, which makes the killing appear more of an everyday, unremarkable incident than it later turns out to have been, sets the right tone of gratuitous violence for Celie's early vision of the world. Celie's later letters grow in fluency, in telling use of detail and in grasp of motive, but she remains an uncomplicated, straightforward narrator. Comparison of Letter 1 and Letter 47 shows how her style develops. Our impression of crudity on first reading the third paragraph of Letter 1 is dispelled as soon as we sense the limits of the girl's vocabulary and understanding. The blunt description conveys exactly the emotion the author wants. Letter 47 puts the same incident into an adult context. In bed with Shug, Celie relives the misery in detail, recalling how the dripping blood 'mess up' her stocking. There is an intimacy and an air of integrity about Celie's odd grammar in such passages: she remembers 'how much I was surprise' by the rape, and here her dialect helps to make her real in our imagination.

In more complex sentences in later letters, we are more likely to notice how slightly the dialect diverges from standard English, and sense the author's contrivance. 'Us' always stands for 'we'. Present tense forms often substitute for others. Conjugation, especially of 'be' and 'have', is jumbled. The final 's' is often used incorrectly ('two mens', 'she say'). Old forms common in many dialects occur, such as 'ain't' for 'am/is/are not', but these are few. There are occasions where it seems Walker has written standard sentences and then adjusted them, by inserting these changes, into Celie's way of talking. (See the first page of Letter 74, for example.) On the whole, Celie's later style is an effective compromise between a richer dialect, which we would not readily understand, and implausibly 'good' English.

Celie is always a lively writer. She uses figurative language, but not too much. Questions run through her mind 'like snakes' (Letter 15). When Shug first appears, seriously ill but flamboyant as usual, Celie says, 'She look like she ain't long for this world but dressed well for the next' (Letter 22). She says of Shug's sharp tongue, 'her mouth just pack with claws' (Letter 24). Later Shug 'smile, like a razor opening' (Letter 27). Celie describes things well too: Shug's 'long black body with it black plum nipples, look like her mouth' (Letter 24); Shug is also 'skinny as a bean, and her face full of eyes' (Letter 27). Good touches such as these are beyond the better-educated but uninspired Nettie.

Dialogue is vigorous and convincing in Celie's letters. Albert may be a weak man, but he has an ear for strong sentence rhythm, as we hear when he denounces the errant Celie:

Look at you. You black, you pore, you ugly, you a woman. Goddam, he say, you nothing at all. (Letter 75)

Steven Spielberg's film weakens this by removing 'Goddam', the word Albert pauses on in feigned surprise at just what a nothing his wife is, and the strong, rising note before the dismissive fall of the voice in 'you nothing at all'. Albert and Alphonso tend to reveal their contemptuous attitudes towards women as much in what is unsaid as in their shameless pronouncements. 'I got a fresh one in there myself', Alphonso tells Albert in Letter 7, referring to his young wife, a virgin when he married her. The novel shows its author's knowledge of the oral folk culture of the old South, on which all speakers can draw. When Celie tells Albert how she has coaxed the ailing Shug into eating some breakfast, and says that nobody living can resist the smell of home-cured ham, she adds, 'If they dead they got a chance. Maybe' (Letter 25). Albert laughs, in a good mood for once because he is relieved about Shug. He and Celie have heard the joke, in the same words, many times; and so has Alice Walker.

It is natural that the well-trained schoolteacher, Nettie, should have abandoned the language of this culture, adopting the competent, dull prose of her school-books. It is a pity in this colourful novel, however, that she should employ so very grey a style. Her letters come as a change and perhaps a relief after Celie's, which, at best, are like urgent dispatches from a battlefront. Nettie's compositions remind us of articles in a missionary-society's magazine. Some seem longer than necessary and lack the vivacity of Celie's unique style.

Characters

Celie

'I have always been a good girl', Celie tells God in the novel's first line. She grows in the course of the story from the pitiful child of the opening pages to the sensible, happy woman of the last. Although always vulnerable, she is steadfast; although often abused, she is loving; when loved, she is able to respond, and to grow. It is difficult to create a good heroine (or hero) in fiction and to retain the reader's respect, especially when the character tells her own story. Alice Walker has succeeded with the character of Celie. She has aimed to create something more than a credible portrait of a good woman, however. In Celie, she tries to present the emancipation of a woman, body and soul, from the domination of men. In the first letters, Celie is almost entirely in the power of Alphonso and Albert. In the last, she is wholly independent of men, a free woman. The idea of Celie as a free woman is more radical and feminist than the traditional idea of a good girl and good woman, but in this portrayal goodness and emancipation go together, and the novelist's success with the character supports the arguments she puts forward.

Celie, the sorry waif who writes to God because there is no one else to pay attention, is not without dignity. She does not understand the meaning of Alphonso's abuse of her. Raped, beaten, deprived of her babies, and of her mother, who dies 'cussing' her, she frets about Nettie, not herself. Walker's art gives her strength without sentimentality:

> I see him looking at my little sister. She scared. But I say I'll take care of you. With God help. (Letter 3)

These words are dignified because, after the horror of Letter 1, they are so restrained. 'I'll take care' sounds brave in such hopeless circumstances, and God is a familiar person in these early pages. The poignancy of Celie 'dressing trampy' in order to entice 'Pa' makes her self-sacrifice to save Nettie vivid and memorable (Letter 7). The scene where Albert sits on his horse and 'inspects' Celie with a view to marriage (Letter 8), and the scene of her efforts on her wedding night to control and clean Albert's children, her head bleeding from a stone Harpo threw, are equally effective (Letter 9). Most of those who rule over Celie's life are brutal, but they cannot brutalise her. Alice Walker shows the resilience of her heroine's good nature in these and many other sensitively written scenes in the early letters. These include the meeting with Corrine in the store, in Letter 10, and her receipt of the surly but trusting confidences of the love-stricken, teenage Harpo, in Letter 13.

It is an especially good touch to make Celie advise Harpo to beat Sofia. It is true to the fact of life that the oppressed tend to accept the thinking of those who oppress them. It is also a redeeming moment of weakness, averting the danger that Celie might become too good to be true. She is not a saint: she has resented Sofia's pitying glances. Our knowledge that Harpo is sure to get the worst of a fight with Sofia adds a comic aspect to stop us disapproving too much of Celie's disloyalty, and her conscience also exacts a penance in the form of insomnia.

Two relationships dominate Celie's life. Her love for Nettie, rooted in childhood loyalties, is more of a bond because of their need to support each other in the face of Alphonso's tyranny. Love of Nettie is akin to love of God in Celie's mind. She breaks off her letters to him only when she has to write to Nettie. Neither distance nor death (when she thinks that Nettie may have died) can diminish the strength of the sisterly bond. Celie's unyielding quality and her gentler virtues arise from this devotion. Her other great passion, for Shug Avery, is very different. This relationship teaches her how to be free.

Celie is sexually attracted to women, and not to men. She tells us in Letter 5 that she looks at women because she is not afraid of them. She tells Albert in Letter 84 that naked men look to her 'like frogs'. She scarcely notices and does not tell us that Albert is a handsome man, as we learn from Corrine in Letter 10; she finds no sexual pleasure or satisfaction in marriage. The novel implies that early abuse has killed her heterosexuality; that certainly helps to explain her longing for security and comfort in the love of a woman. Shug captivates her from the first glimpse, in a photograph (Letter 6). Dressed to kill, and with serious, sad eyes, the Shug of the photograph occupies Celie's fantasies: in devilry and independence, beauty and glamour, Shug is all she cannot be herself. At a particularly bad moment, Celie looks in Shug's eyes in the picture and reads there, 'Yeah, it *bees* that way sometimes', words of comfort (Letter 7). Shug's presence in the neighbourhood thrills Celie, in Letter 14; and a dream seems to have come true (as often happens in this novel) when she becomes Shug's nurse (Letter 24). The strong sexual attraction is announced here without fuss. Looking at Shug's body, Celie thinks she has 'turned into a man'. Shug's dedication of a song is a proud moment, in Letter 33. It is in Letter 35 that Shug begins to teach her about sexual pleasure, but it is not until twelve letters and many years later that they make love on a night when Albert and Grady are out drinking.

The two attachments of her life are now connected, since Shug the lover promptly discovers Nettie the missing sister by finding the letters with 'funny' stamps (Letter 50). Rage at Albert's theft combines with confidence drawn from her lover to enable Celie to defy, curse and leave Albert – 'Now I know Nettie alive I begin to strut a little', she says (Letter 61). She struts more as the novel moves to its close. One turning point is Letter 67 where she learns that Alphonso is not her father or Nettie's, and another is Letter 74 where she tells Albert he is a 'lowdown dog'.

Shug gives Celie many kinds of freedom. She frees her from the concept of God as an old white man, and teaches her to believe in the Spirit that unites our inner life with the power that made the universe and the colour purple. She backs 'Folkspants, Unlimited', a symbol of emancipation. (Symbolism aside, we may think it is Celie's money, partly derived from Folkspants, that enables her to chat with Albert in the last chapters as an equal of sorts.) It could be said that Shug strengthens Celie further by leaving her to go off with Germaine. Celie will always be vulnerable, but in Letter 89 she has learned to accept that Shug is a free spirit with a life of her own. By the time of the last letter, she deserves to be made happy.

Shug Avery

Shug is as remarkable as the story requires. Her parents called her Lillie but she turned out to be (to all her admirers) the Queen Honeybee, or Sugar or Shug. 'She just so sweet they call her Shug', Celie says (Letter 50). She can be sweet when she performs as a professional blues singer. At other times, as Celie says, 'her mouth just pack with claws' (Letter 24). She succeeds as a singer, and so gets rich, because she can dominate an audience, and she dominates her lovers too. It may have been rebellion against her strange mother, who loathed all physical contact with others, that made her sensual, independent and strong-willed. She sometimes surprises herself by how ruthless she can be, as when she tells Celie how cruel she was to Annie Julia when this unfortunate woman was made to marry Albert: 'I was so mean and wild'; and she regrets having treated Celie with disdain, 'like you was a servant', at the time of her illness (Letter 50). She loves Albert because he is so 'funny' and 'little', and because he could make her laugh in the old days, but she has never wanted to marry him – only to make sure he prefers her over all other women. She marries the foolish, toothy Grady, and pays for his car while ordering him about, as she orders Albert, and later spends a few months with the attractive nineteen-year-old Germaine, who pleases her for a while. She loves men with passion, as she often says, but she does not intend to be subject to any man. It may be that she has a masculine element in her nature. Celie observes that she often speaks like a man, especially when commenting on girls (Letter 36). She is kind to Celie, staying on at Albert's to make sure he stops beating her, and to Mary Agnes, whom she helps become a singer, but she enjoys her power over them both.

She is a free spirit in every realm. Celie thinks her too 'evil' to submit to illness for long (Letter 23). She is too restless to stay long at home with anyone – to the regret of Celie and Albert. She has a good, opinionated mind, and seems to have thought out her own unorthodox views. She takes her bisexual nature for granted and enjoys it. She is free of the fear of God, although she checks Celie's 'blasphemous' talk in Letter 73. Some of her religious notions are vague, but she is quite sure God is not male. She sounds almost facetious when she speaks the lines in Letter 73 that give the book its title. It could be said in her defence that she is serious about God but not about the solemn religious terms that men have invented.

Where many characters are strictly regional figures, who think of Memphis as a great city, Shug is at home everywhere. In creating her, Alice Walker had in mind the great blues singers, including Bessie Smith, said in Letter 33 to have been a friend of Shug's. Some readers may regret that we do not hear more about the people Shug must have known and talked with in California and New York.

Sofia

Sofia is a contrast to Celie. A brutal upbringing has made her a fighter. She has had to fight off her father, brothers and cousins: 'A girl child ain't safe in a family of men.' Her father hated children, and women too. Her mother was kept 'under my daddy foot' (Letter 21). Big and strong, she and her sisters learned to hit back, and Sofia now does so as a reflex action. She batters Harpo when he tries to inflict what he considers a required marital beating. She knocks down Mary Agnes, when slapped by this smaller girl; and she knocks down the white mayor when he slaps her. The ferocious beating she receives from the police forces her to submit to the prison regime for the first three years of her twelve-year sentence, and then to the humiliating condition of prisoner-maid, a kind of slavery, in the mayor's household. In spite of all this ill-treatment, she remains a formidable woman when released.

Sofia is very strong-minded, instinctively rejecting all the conventional ideas about a woman's role that her culture and society so firmly assert. She takes naturally to various 'manly' activities, including heavy outdoor work. Far from 'minding' Harpo, she takes all domestic decisions, such as when to take the children to visit her sisters. She does love Harpo, although she is unwilling to obey him. If only Harpo would forget about trying to rule her, it seems that they would be well-matched, in a marriage freed from stereotyped roles, because he likes cooking and caring for the children. When she leaves Harpo, however, she chooses a man who looks like a prize-fighter; it is not clear how we are meant to interpret that.

Sofia is a character who sometimes plays a comic role, but suffers a tragic fate. We may be amused when Harpo talks about his injuries from the barn-door and cantankerous mule; but when we hear, in Celie's recounting of Sofia's downfall, that the mayor has slapped her, we share Mary Agnes's horror at what is going to happen next to this woman of fighting spirit, in a society such as hers. That she survives her sufferings and imprisonment, and ends the novel as a dignified and courageous woman, is a symbol of the triumph of good over evil.

Mary Agnes/'Squeak'

Mary Agnes is foremost among the minor female characters. Her role is reflected in the alternation of her name and nickname. As Squeak, she is a jukejoint girl: small, light ('yellow')-skinned, and docile, she frequents Harpo's bar and becomes attached to him in the absence of Sofia. Her smallness and high-pitched voice make her a figure of fun in this milieu. When Celie persuades her to claim her proper name and be Mary Agnes, she gains at once in dignity, choosing a most dramatic moment, immediately after her visit to the prison warden, to do so. As Mary Agnes, she has the self-confidence to become a singer, although she seems to relapse somewhat in Grady's company, but at the end of the story she is independent once more, preparing to tour the north of the country with her new songs. She contributes to the theme of solidarity among women, in her instant concern for Sofia in Letter 37, and in helping to look after Sofia's children later on.

Albert/Mr. ——

Albert is known to Celie as Mr. —— until the final letter, when she accepts him as 'family', although not as a husband. It is not until Letter 89 that she acknowledges his name. Like Alphonso, and most men, it is implied, in this community, he lacks all respect for women. He looks on his second marriage as the acquisition of two pieces of property, Celie and a cow, the latter being the greater asset. The beatings and insults he inflicts on Celie combined with his indifference to his children, and his idleness, make him a man to be despised. He is a fairly sensual man, callous and childishly petulant, as Shug tells him, but oddly stubborn in hiding the letters for so many years. (It could be argued that this melodramatic aspect of his role does not suit him.) He is fundamentally weak, as some bullies are; he beats Celie because 'she isn't Shug', until Shug makes him stop; he suffers a nervous breakdown when Celie leaves him.

There is another Albert, however. He was loved by Shug in their youth, for his laughter and his dancing, and he has loved Shug ever since. He takes her in when she is sick and in disgrace for wild ways, and grieves over her. Love of Shug gives him feelings in common with Celie, and he begins to be a more attractive character from that point on. But he is only allowed a degree of sympathy. By hiding the letters, he merits Celie's term of abuse; he is a 'lowdown dog' (Letter 74). He speaks the anti-'womanist' manifesto at the heart of the novel: 'You black, you pore, you ugly, you a woman. Goddam, you nothing at all' (Letter 74).

He appears strangely transformed in the last letters, after his breakdown, sewing pants and talking sensibly; this is partly explicable if we consider that his new respect for Celie is based on her newly acquired wealth. But some readers may doubt whether all aspects of this character's behaviour fit together.

Harpo

Albert's son Harpo is to be seen as a good or at least tolerable man who is too stupid to think his way out of his father's precepts about the subjection of women and understand his good fortune in marriage to Sofia. We often sympathise with Harpo. He is to be pitied when he relives the occasion of his mother's murder in a nightmare, and then pleads with Celie: 'It not her fault somebody kill her, he say. It not! It not!' (Letter 17). We may sympathise, too, when Sofia and their children leave him in Letter 28. We may admire him when he rescues Albert from despair; the sight of him asleep and 'holding his daddy in his arms' makes Sofia start to 'feel again for Harpo' at the end of Letter 79. He is attractive in a different way when he recovers his spirits after Sofia's departure and sets up his jukejoint.

At other times, Harpo is a farcical figure of fun: eating six eggs for breakfast, for example, in his effort to become as big and powerful as Sofia (Letter 28). His enjoyment of domestic tasks, child-minding and cooking, complements Sofia's satisfaction in outdoor work. Both characters are intended to demonstrate the author's belief that traditional male and female roles have arisen from social convenience rather than from human nature, and that an insistent belief in these roles can be destructive.

Alphonso

Alphonso says in Letter 69 that May Ellen, a teenage girl when he marries her after the death of Celie's mother in Letter 4, has left him because she 'Got too old for me I reckon.' Her replacement is another child-wife called Daisy. He rapes Celie when she is fourteen and soon afterwards has his eye on the still younger Nettie. He particularly enjoys treating these girls as slaves. Celie is made to cut his hair just before and immediately after his violation of her. Alphonso parades her before Albert and speaks of her as though a slave for sale: 'she ain't fresh' (Letter 7). He deliberately conceals the facts of their parentage from Celie and Nettie, and says in defence that knowledge of their father's fate would have upset them. He also withholds their property. 'Pa' has no redeeming features.

Grady

In Alice Walker's novels, men are (in general) the weaker sex, although not the gentler. Albert, Harpo, Alphonso and Grady exemplify male weakness and male impulses to bully. Like Harpo, Grady is to be seen as a thoughtless man who repeats unthinkingly the common opinions of his time and place: 'A woman can't get a man if peoples talk', he says when Celie is leaving home (Letter 74). Everybody laughs at him on that occasion. His red braces and bow ties look vulgar to Celie (because she is jealous of him). To end his days growing marijuana in Panama seems an appropriate fate for him (although not for Mary Agnes who leaves him there and returns to sing and look after her daughter).

Samuel and Adam

The Reverend Samuel and his son Adam are exceptional members of the novel's cast: they are reasonably intelligent and sensible men, and they have a positive attitude towards women. Samuel, indeed, is remarkable in his dedication to missionary work, and wise in dealing with his family. He is tender-hearted in accepting Nettie into his household when he believes her to be the mother of his adopted children. We see and hear very little of them, however, and then only through the medium of Nettie's letters. She praises Samuel first as a protector and later as a husband; she praises Adam first as a pleasant boy, later as a principled young man and the lover of Tashi; but she does not attempt to bring them to life with scenes of dialogue and action of the sort that make Albert and Harpo so vivid and memorable.

Nettie and Corrine

Netttie has all the good qualities necessary for a missionary, a schoolteacher and a maiden aunt. She is a conscientious girl at school. She remains dutiful and earnest throughout the novel, also possessing enough tact to survive in her awkward position in Samuel's family without losing his affection or respect, or the love of the children. She shares with Celie remarkable stamina. Her letters reveal a sympathetic observer of the African setting, appropriately prim. We are bound to take Nettie's side, but we may also feel sorry for Corrine, whose jealousy is understandable and whose death is required by the story (since another good man for Nettie to marry might be hard to find). Nettie and Corrine have taught Olivia the progressive, liberal American views which Olivia passes on to Tashi. Tashi's difficulties, placed between the missionaries and her own people, are outlined in Nettie's letters, but remain in the distant background of the story.

Part 4

Hints for study

The film

The film *The Color Purple* (1985), directed by Steven Spielberg, is of obvious interest to students of the novel, but it also presents some dangers to examinees, because it differs from Alice Walker's book in a number of respects.

The acting is good throughout, and some scenes are both effective and closely modelled on what happens in the novel. These include Sofia's hitting the mayor and Miss Millie's attempt to take Sofia home for Christmas. Other scenes are very convincing, but alter the novel's action and timing of events. Celie's encounter with Corrine in the store, for example, shows us what a shop in the old South would have looked like, and lets us hear the rude voice of the white 'clerk', but the child Olivia, six years old in the book, is a baby. A dramatic sequence in the film alternates shots of Celie standing behind Albert with his razor in her hand with shots of Adam and Olivia undergoing the ceremony of ritual scarring in Africa. The circumstances in each case are changed from those of the novel: Celie is not required to shave Albert in the novel, and Shug is in the room with them, while on the screen she races across the fields to stop Celie; Olivia and Adam are scarred as children in the film, as adults in the novel. Olivia and Adam undergo the ritual on separate occasions in the book, and years after the time when Celie wants to kill Albert.

However, many of the film's changes seem fully justified. Much detail has to be omitted from the film; a single image on the screen can replace an effect contrived over many pages. Serious novelists have always tended to find that film-treatments involve other alterations with a view to winning the biggest popular success. There are changes of these kinds throughout Spielberg's film. Alice Walker was employed as a consultant on the film, but authors' contracts for such consultancies do not often allow them a decisive say in the process of adaptation, and rightly not, because making films and writing novels are different arts.

Much of the sexual violence described in the novel is omitted on the screen. The rape of Celie reported in the first letter is not shown in the film, which opens with Celie and Nettie romping happily in the fields; the horrific facts of the case so boldly stated in the text are shyly and briefly murmured, and could easily be missed by a cinema-goer whose ear was not yet attuned to Celie's drawl. The continual beatings of the novel are also left out. Celie's hard labour in squalid conditions during her early years with Albert is also omitted or much subdued. Walker's Celie is in rags when Albert's sisters visit her; Spielberg's is always nicely dressed. Domestic life in the film is too cosy. Conventional Hollywood scenes such as Albert's trying to cook Shug's breakfast occupy more time than episodes of greater interest, such as the whole marital struggle of Harpo and Sofia. The love affair between Celie and Shug is not shown (or said) to include sexual relations, except for a few kisses. The feminist themes and the strictures on colonialism in Africa are considerably muted. The film's Africa is one of elephants, giraffes and vaguely-pictured tribesmen, in a different physical setting from the one Walker describes. Spielberg elaborates on the religious element, however, making use of church choirs.

The result was a very successful film. *The Color Purple* won seven awards and eleven Academy Award nominations. It is well worth watching more than once. Candidates for examinations in English literature must be very careful, however, if they watch the film, to keep the novel apart in their minds. However well we think we know a book, the potency of the cinema can trick us into remembering as a part of the text some image or detail from a film version. That can be fatal in an examination. Candidates must guard against it; and if the film is to be mentioned in an answer, differences in action and interpretation must be fully explained.

Preparing to answer questions

Texts for further reading are recommended in Part 5. Reading more works of literature is better than spending a lot of time on critical studies (although it is interesting to dip into these occasionally). It is a good idea to sample a variety of novels that are not required reading but have a bearing on the set book. These might include one or two other novels by Alice Walker (or some of her short stories), novels by other women writers from the American South, and some African novels in English. Use a notebook for points of comparison with *The Color Purple*. Background reading ought to be a pleasure. Allow for the fact that good books often require some effort before a reader's bearings can be found; but then discard a dull novel and try another.

Background reading should not interfere with close study of the set text. This must be read repeatedly and explored as thoroughly as possible. Plentiful and exact details from the text, used to illustrate the points in your answers, impress examiners. Revision projects which involve searching the text help to sharpen detailed knowledge. A study of the minor characters might be such a project. Try to identify these: Tobias, Odessa, Bubber Hodges, Joseph, May Ellen, Daisy, Jerene and Darlene, Suzie Q, Billy, Miss Beasley, James, Swain, 'Buster' and Jack. They are worth mentioning by name, if the opportunity arises in an answer, and the search for them will improve close knowledge of the book. Names must be carefully memorised: Beasley, not Beasly; Millie, not Milly. It is good exercise to hunt for them: when do we learn Celie's name, Albert's name, Alphonso's name, Shug's original name, Olivia's other name? Another project might deal with ages: these tend to be approximate, although the novel occasionally tells us one. Pursuing ages may provoke thoughts about the novel's structure. Try to work out: Celie's age when she nurses Shug; Sofia's age when she leaves Harpo; Nettie's age when she goes to Africa; Albert's age when he marries Celie; the ages of Adam and Tashi when they marry. Investigate clothes: who wears what and when? Clothes carry all sorts of significance in literature as well as life. Investigate transport. How do the characters travel? What does Nettie notice about her journey to Africa? What does Celie notice about cars and roads?

The more you write the better. There is a big difference between passive knowledge and active performance, between what you understand and what you can readily put into words. It is a bad mistake to spend long periods reading and note-taking and then go into an examination without practice in writing. Writing helps to clarify ideas and to produce new ones. Practise writing short essays without books or notes. *Preparing for Examinations in English Literature*, in the York Handbooks series, gives further advice. Two last points are essential. (1) Quotations must be accurate, short and relevant. (2) Everything in an examination essay must be related to answering the question. Never just 'tell the story': each paragraph must make a point, supported by examples from the story.

Some essay topics and specimen answers are given below.

Some specimen questions

(1) Consider *The Color Purple* as a feminist novel.
(2) Discuss the novel's presentation of religious faith.
(3) How closely can the novel's events be dated?
(4) Discuss Celie's relationship with Shug.
(5) Discuss Sofia's relationship with Harpo.
(6) Discuss the role of Albert (Mr. ——).
(7) Discuss the presentation of white people.
(8) What do we learn about Africa in the colonial period in this novel?
(9) What do we learn about America in the earlier twentieth century?
(10) '*The Color Purple* depicts many scenes of violence, but it is a tender novel.' Do you agree?
(11) Are Celie and Nettie alike? In what ways are they different?
(12) In what ways does the use of letters contribute to the novel's unity and effectiveness?
(13) Trace the changes in Celie's relationship with her husband.
(14) How do you think Albert might try to defend his treatment of Celie

and how might he explain that the failure of their marriage is inevitable?

(15) Explain the novel's title.

(16) Discuss language and style in *The Color Purple*.

(17) Why does Albert hide Nettie's letters instead of destroying them?

(18) What problems are Adam and Tashi likely to face if they settle in the southern United States?

(19) Consider the roles of some of the minor characters, such as Miss Millie, Eleanor Jane, Grady, Odessa and Olivia.

(20) Write a short, detailed essay on one or more of the following with relation to *The Color Purple*: purple; children; meals; singing; clothes; quilt-making.

Specimen answers

(1) Consider *The Color Purple* as a feminist novel.

Feminist is the customary term, but we should bear in mind that Alice Walker prefers the term 'womanist' for a black feminist – commenting that 'womanist is to feminist as purple is to lavender', darker and stronger too. Walker's purpose in this novel is to show the ill-treatment black women have suffered in the past, especially in the recent history of the southern United States but also in Africa, and to show how they have struggled to achieve their freedom. Their hardships and humiliations have been such that Zora Neale Hurston, the black woman novelist Walker most reveres, called them 'the mules of the world'. Their creative gifts were stifled for generations, and Walker's essay, 'In Search of Our Mothers' Gardens', tells how her sense of that loss is the source of her inspiration.

The theme of emancipation is present throughout *The Color Purple*. Celie and Nettie are all but enslaved, in the opening stages of the story, to men who are their intellectual and moral inferiors. By the end they have achieved dignity, independence and the power of self-expression; Nettie as a wife and a teacher, Celie as a clothes-designer and business woman needing no husband. Sofia is imprisoned for nearly twelve years, and labours during the days for much of this time as a servant to the white woman, Miss Millie, who has provoked her trifling offence. (She speaks without the required deference to Miss Millie, and hits back when slapped by her husband, the mayor and a white man.) The injustice of white supremacy in the old South is forcefully demonstrated, here and elsewhere in the novel, but more space and emphasis is given to men's injustice to women, regardless of race. Sofia would have been at home with Harpo except for his absurd longing for his wife's total obedience. In contrast to these victims of oppression, Shug Avery is a heroic figure, in Celie's eyes a queen deserving the colour purple, because she has won her independence and will never be any man's 'mule'. She sings as she lives, boldly; and is indifferent to 'how people talk'. Like Sofia, she has learned to fight, but more effectively without using her fists, and she teaches Celie to do the same.

Celie learns, gradually. We see her courage in Letter 3, when she vows to save Nettie from the man she thinks is her father, but this is courage on behalf of her beloved younger sister. She has no opinion of her own worth, not even signing her letters. She actually sacrifices herself to save Nettie in Letter 7; she is always inclined to do so, meekly marrying Mr. ——, as she calls Albert, and toiling in his house and fields, as though resolved to live her life as a 'mule'. We can see that she hankers for a better life, however, in the envy of Sofia's independence that makes her tell Harpo to beat his wife, and in her love of Shug Avery.

The novel asserts that all women are sisters. Comforted and made to feel secure by Shug, Celie is ready to fight Albert when the discovery of the letters reveals the depth of his guilt. Only Shug can restrain her then from murdering him. When she first curses and then leaves Albert, Shug gives her a home in Memphis and helps her to launch 'Folkspants, Unlimited', a firm that symbolises her newfound freedom by selling pants (especially purple ones) for women. Shug also teaches her friend a new conception of God, one not subject to the image of a white man. The scene described in Letter 74, just after that conversation about religion, shows Celie, Shug, Sofia and Mary Agnes (who has already proved her sisterhood with Sofia), uniting to assert their independence from the men.

Men are at their worst in this feminist novel. There is a background chorus of male grumbling about the inferiority of the sex they assume to be weaker. The chorus is largely composed of buffoons such as Alphonso, Albert, Harpo and the white mayor. Harpo has been taught his privileged position in life (and, it seems, little else): 'Women work, I'm a man', he says when still a boy and asked by Albert's sister Kate to do some chores (Letter 12). Albert teaches Harpo that women have to be beaten because they are like children; but men are the childish ones, in their actions, throughout the story. When Albert is left alone, he has to be comforted like a child by his son. The women retaliate with small acts of defiance. Sofia says Harpo wants a dog rather than a wife, and she leaves him. Celie comes, in time, to sound like a womanist; 'wherever there's a man, there's trouble', she tells Nettie, reversing the old saying. When Squeak declares herself Mary Agnes, this too is a gesture of rebellion, since the nickname arose in the men's world of the jukejoint. Even the sisters' letter-writing is defiant, since women's literacy was discouraged in the old South.

Nettie's letters from Africa reinforce the theme that the world is changing. Nettie tells Tashi's father that 'it is no longer a world just for boys and men'. Tashi manages to go to school, in spite of her father's attitude, and as times goes by other girls follow. Nettie's remark that African men are like children is a serious comment, while Albert's remark about women is a stale and thoughtless piece of contempt. Olivia is thoughtful, too, saying that Africans who want to keep girls from going to school are like white racialists in America. This remark is one of many that interconnect the African and American parts of the book, and reaffirm its message that black women, long oppressed, have learned to fight together for their freedom.

---

(2) Discuss the novel's presentation of religious faith.

The Color Purple is dedicated to 'the Spirit', and fifty-six of its ninety letters are written by Celie to God. It is clear that spiritual life is a theme in this novel, but how far does it characterise the book? Religious thoughts and feelings are often expressed in Celie's and Nettie's letters. Nettie is a missionary, living with a dedicated Christian family. She depends on God in her daily struggle through a hard life as an often lonely woman. Shug Avery possesses her own, rather different creed, and converts Celie to her idea of the Spirit. A change in spiritual life accompanies Celie's emancipation. These elements are pervasive, but not central, however. This novel is dominated by one passionate commitment, to the rights of black women. It would be misleading to call it 'a religious novel'. It is a womanist or black feminist novel, although religion has a crucial place in Walker's idea of a womanist.

The story shows how Celie tries to live by an old type of belief, and how it fails her. The novel argues that it fails because its doctrines are out-moded, derived from a world meant only for men and chiefly for white men. While she is a child and a young woman, Celie's faith is simple and absolute. God is her only friend, besides her sister. Her trust adds to the emotional impact of the earliest letters. She speaks as she has heard others when she tells her mother, in Letter 2, that God has taken her baby. When she says goodbye to Nettie in Letter 11, she says that as 'long as I can spell G-o-d I got somebody along.' She quotes the Bible to the bellicose Sofia in Letter 21: 'Honour father and mother no matter what', a gruesome touch on Walker's part. This life is short, she says like millions of poor people before her, black and white: 'Heaven last all ways'. When Sofia is in prison, Celie dreams of 'God coming down by chariot, swinging down real low and carrying ole Sofia home' (Letter 39). Her words echo the language and rhythm of the spirituals she sings in church.

This close, trusting relationship with God ends abruptly when Celie learns (in Letter 67) that Alphonso is not her real father. She feels betrayed because God seems to have made a fool of her, as she says in Letter 68: 'My daddy lynch. My mamma crazy . . . Pa not pa. You must be asleep.' This is her last letter to God until Letter 90. She says God seems like a man, 'Trifling, forgitful and lowdown' (Letter 73). But now Shug speaks her mind, telling her that God is not the old white man in the sky she has always pictured, and not the God of church-going believers. God is not to be thought of as 'he' but as 'it', pleased with its creation of everything, including the colour purple in a field of flowers, and if people do not notice the wonder of creation ' it pisses God off'. The same Spirit resides within. Celie thinks this at first 'blasphemy sure nuff'. Later her religious faith revives, in this new form.

Nettie's letters give her some support. Nettie has always known that God is Spirit, but Africa has freed her and Samuel from the need to picture him in any particular way. He may be thought of in terms of Christian imagery or as in Olinka belief where roofleaf is divine. They are somewhat estranged, too, from organised religion. The missionaries seem to have failed in Africa. White clergy are cold and aloof. Nettie is ready to join Celie at the close in speaking to God and all people and Everything in a single prayer of thanks. All that is good, the novel appears to say, reflects the Spirit, unmoralising, unconfined by doctrine, and definitely unmale.

---

(3) How closely can the novel's events be dated?

None of the letters are dated in the novel; Celie does not record the dates she finds on Nettie's letters. Some letters tell us how many years have passed since the one before; others do not. There is sometimes a vagueness about the passage of time. This is natural: neither sister is keeping a journal. The use of letters is likely to make some readers inquisitive about dates, and inclined to look out for clues to help connect events to the calendar.

Letter 80 offers an approximate date by referring to the approach of a 'big war'; this must be late in the 1930s. Since at least two years of the war have passed by the time of Nettie's return to America, the date here must be around 1939. The war has started by Letter 85, which is presumably to be dated between 1939 and 1941. Nettie gives a useful clue in Letter 86 by saying that it is nearly thirty years since she last saw Celie, implying a date around 1912 for their parting in Letter 11. Working back from there, we may suppose that Celie marries Albert in 1911, since they have not been together long when Nettie comes to live with them, and her need to escape from Alphonso is urgent once Celie's protection is removed. Letter 10 reports the meeting with Corrine where Olivia is said to be six years old; this means that Letter 1 belongs to the period 1904–5. Celie must have been born about 1890.

We can try to work forward from the date of Celie's marriage. Harpo is then twelve (Letter 9). He is seventeen in Letter 13 when he first talks about Sofia; this must be about 1916. So far he has only managed to wink at Sofia in church; when they marry, her first baby is 'a big ole nursing boy', so we must allow at least another year: Letter 18 belongs to 1917 or

1918. The next letter says that Harpo and Sofia have been married three years, bringing us to about 1920; it is at least 1921 when she leaves him because they now have five children. This is about the time of Shug Avery's arrival, sick, to stay with Albert and Celie. Since the restless Shug stays on only to persuade Albert to stop beating Celie, after her recovery, Sofia's return ought not to be more than two years later; Shug is still singing at Harpo's place then. 1924 must be the approximate date for the events of Letters 37–41 (covering Sofia's imprisonment). Letter 43 says that Sofia was in prison for three years before starting to work as a maid for Miss Millie. We are now in 1927. Two more years of Sofia's sentence have passed by Letter 44: 1929.

Shug's return at Christmas in the next letter is difficult to date. It must be some years after Letter 44, although no mention is made of the passage of time. It is during this visit that Celie and Shug find the letters from Nettie. The first letter from Nettie that Celie reads says that the family are already planning to return to America. We must be well into the 1930s. That is confirmed by the fact that Sofia has been released from prison after eleven and a half years of her sentence, as we know from Letter 74 where Celie is still angry with Albert about his suppression of the correspondence. This is 1935 or 1936.

Nettie's encounter with Sofia, described in Letter 55, is impossible to date, if we accept this scheme. Sofia is working as Miss Millie's maid, which means a date on or after 1927. Nettie is about to leave for Africa, and is persuaded to go by this meeting. But Olivia and Adam would be adults by this time, and they are plainly young children when first in Africa. Letters 52–5 show that Nettie leaves for Africa soon after her parting from Celie, which is about 1912. Letter 52 is written just after Nettie's flight, and the next says that it is too soon to hope for a reply. By Letter 54, Nettie is 'almost crazy' at having had no reply. but it is clear that weeks, or just possibly months, have passed, not years. Letter 55 tells us in a headnote from Celie (unique in referring to a date) that it is dated two months after the last, and Nettie is now writing from Africa.

There are other odd features of the time-scheme. Adam and Tashi are in their thirties when they marry, about 1941, yet they behave as though at an earlier stage of life. Events among the Olinka do not seem to fit such a long span of years as the novel requires. It is best to keep the calendar roughly in mind, but not to worry about it pedantically.

Part 5

Suggestions for further reading

Works by Alice Walker

All published in New York by Harcourt Brace Jovanovich, and in London by The Women's Press.

Novels: *The Third Life of Grange Copeland*, 1970; *Meridian*, 1976; *The Color Purple*, 1982; *The Temple of My Familiar*, 1989.

Short stories: *In Love and Trouble: Stories of Black Women*, 1973; *You Can't Keep a Good Woman Down: Stories*, 1981.

Verse: *Once: Poems*, 1968; *Revolutionary Petunias*, 1973; *Good Night, Willie Lee, I'll See You in the Morning*, 1979; *Horses Make a Landscape Look More Beautiful*, 1984.

Essays and criticism: *Langston Hughes: American Poet*, 1974; *In Search of Our Mothers' Gardens: Womanist Prose*, 1983; *Living by the Word: Selected Writings 1983–87*, 1988.

American fiction by black women

HURSTON, ZORA NEALE: *Mules and Men* (1935), Negro University Press, New York, 1969.
———: *Their Eyes Were Watching God* (1937), Virago Press, London, 1986.
———: *I Love Myself When I Am Laughing: A Zora Neale Hurston Reader*, ed. Alice Walker, Feminist Press, New York, 1979.
MARSHALL, PAULE: *Brown Girl, Brownstones*, Random House, New York, 1959; W. H. Allen, London, 1960.
———: *The Chosen Place, The Timeless People*, Harcourt Brace Jovanovich, New York, 1969; Longman, London, 1970.
———: *Praisesong for the Widow*, Putnam's, New York, 1983.
MORRISON, TONI: *The Bluest Eye*, Pocket Books, New York, 1970; Panther Books, London, 1981.
———: *Sula*, Knopf, New York, 1973; Chatto & Windus, London, 1980.
———: *Tar Baby*, Knopf, New York, 1981; Chatto & Windus, London, 1981.
WALKER, MARGARET: *Come Down from Yonder Mountain*, Longman, Toronto, 1962.
———: *Jubilee*, Houghton Mifflin, Boston, 1965.

WASHINGTON, MARY HELEN (*ed.*): *Black-Eyed Susans: Classic Stories By and About Black Women*, Anchor Press, New York, 1975.

African novels in English

ACHEBE, CHINUA: *Things Fall Apart*, Heinemann, London, 1958.
——: *Arrow of God*, Heinemann, London, 1964.
AMADI, ELECHI: *The Concubine*, Heinemann, London, 1966.
HEAD, BESSIE: *When Rain Clouds Gather*, Gollancz, London, 1968.
——: *Maru*, Gollancz, London, 1971.
——: *A Question of Power*, Davis-Poynter, London, 1974.

Criticism

BARTHOLD, BONNIE J.: *Black Time: Fiction of Africa, the Caribbean and the United States*, Yale University Press, New Haven, 1981.
BONE, ROBERT: *The Negro Novel in America*, revised edition, Yale University Press, New Haven, 1965.
CHRISTIAN, BARBARA: Black Women Novelists: The Development of a Tradition 1892–1976, Greenwood Press, Westport, 1980.
EVANS, MARI (*ed.*): *Black Women Writers: A Critical Evaluation*, Anchor Press, New York, 1984. Includes an article on Alice Walker by Bettie J. Parker-Smith.
McEWAN, NEIL: *Africa and the Novel*, Macmillan, London, 1983.
O'BRIEN, JOHN (*ed.*): *Interviews with Black Writers*, Liveright Press, New York, 1973; includes an interview with Alice Walker.
PRENSHAWE, PEGGY WHITMAN: *Writers of the Contemporary South*, Mississippi University Press, Jackson, 1984.
PRYSE, MARJORIE and SPILLERS, HORTENSE J.: *Conjuring: Black Women, Fiction, and Literary Tradition*, Indiana University Press, Bloomington, 1985.

The author of these notes

NEIL MCEWAN read English at Pembroke College, Oxford, and has taught English Literature at the Universities of Alberta, Leeds, Yaounde, Fez, and Qatar. He now teaches in the English Department at Okayama University, Japan. He has published several critical studies, including *The Survival of the Novel*, *Africa and the Novel*, *Perspective in British Historical Fiction Today*; and *Graham Greene* and *Anthony Powell* in the 'Macmillan Modern Novelists' series. He edited Volume 5, *The Twentieth Century*, in the *Macmillan Anthologies of English Literature*. His many contributions to York Notes include *D. H. Lawrence: Selected Short Stories* (1991).